The HAPPIEST MUSICIAN

How to Thrive in Your Creative Career

JENNET INGLE

The Happiest Musician: How to Thrive in Your Creative Career
by Jennet Ingle

Published by Jennet Ingle

For permissions contact: jennet@jennetingle.com

www.jennetingle.com

Cover and interior design by Steve Peha

Cover design inspired by the work of Pamela Colman Smith

Foreword by Elizabeth Rowe

ISBN: 979-8-9854388-0-2 (print)

Printed in the United States

First Edition, December 2021

DEDICATION

For the musicians, the creatives, the dreamers and doers who want to see their whole lives as one big YES, AND.

I love you all. Stay safe out there.

TABLE OF CONTENTS

Foreword

By Elizabeth Rowe,
Principal Flutist, Boston Symphony Orchestra

The very title of this book is a bit radical, isn't it? At least to outsiders looking in, it's easy to assume that *of course* professional musicians are happy. We must be—we're doing the thing we love most in the world... and we're getting paid for it!

And yet.

Talk to most professional musicians—everyone from principal players in the very top orchestras to early professionals just starting out—and you'll learn that actually, truly, thriving is by no means a given for most musicians. In fact, it's startlingly rare. I know this because I see it every day in my high-profile orchestra, and because I hear it over and over again in my conversations with musicians in all corners of the industry and all stages of life.

Why is this? What's standing in the way? Here's what I think: Most of us begin playing our instruments at a young age, called to this art form by a pure and innocent love of music. We follow this love into adulthood without ever learning how to place it into the context of an adult life. We never stop to consider that this love—while powerful—might not actually be enough to sustain our adult selves.

"My love of music isn't enough to make me happy."

It's almost sacrilegious to say those words out loud. You *should* be happy if you're doing what you love, right? Or, even if it's a bit of a struggle to be happy right at this very moment, never fear—you'll be happy *once you get a better job.* (After all, most of our teachers taught us that our job defines us, so it follows that the fancier our job is, the happier we'll be.) So you keep putting one foot in front of the other, figuring that eventually you will become "successful," and *then* you'll also become happy... because that's what's supposed to happen.

But what if that big job never materializes—or hasn't yet? What about your happiness today, tomorrow, next year? How long will it take? How long will you wait?

Perhaps you're determined to be a "noble" but impoverished artist, sustained purely by the love of the art form. If that works for you, wonderful! But I'm guessing it doesn't work for most of you. The truth is that while music may indeed feed the soul, a career that feeds the soul but doesn't provide the means to feed your body or care for your sick child is simply not enough. Let's get one thing straight: the desire for financial security doesn't make a person less of an artist. Financial security allows us to exhale, and to find the courage to take those essential risks that make art come alive. Of course money isn't everything—and nobody goes into music to become rich—but a baseline of financial stability is something every human being deserves... including musicians.

But a big job with a stable salary is no guarantee of happiness, either. I know; I have one. My fancy title doesn't protect me from my ongoing struggles with loneliness, imposter syndrome, and demoralizing structural inequities. The fancy title didn't protect me from making deeply painful personal sacrifices because the demands of the job left me little choice—or at least, that's how it felt to me at the time. The fancy title doesn't make me a good person, a good teacher, or a good friend. It makes me a flutist with a fancy title.

Don't get me wrong: I am privileged. I am highly compensated and I work with world class artists. I know just how lucky I am and how rare my circumstances are. I am grateful, as are many of my colleagues. And yet many of us still struggle to find satisfaction in our lives. We struggle to define our own worth: *Does what I do actually matter? Do I actually matter?* And we wonder what's wrong with us if we don't feel like those happy musicians we're expected to be.

I think we forget that musicians are people, too. There's so much more to us than the music we make. We have relationships, hobbies, families, bodies that need tending to, inner lives that sometimes take up a lot of space. We experience traumas. We can be great with numbers or not! We can be goofy, stubborn, creative, playful, sometimes reserved. We are problem solvers. Some of us are overbearing, some of us are introverts, all of us are entertainers.

In other words, we are multidimensional beings.

But this isn't what we were taught. We were taught that we are defined only by what we do, by what's printed on our résumé. And, further, we were taught that whatever is printed there is what will truly make us happy. And so we strive, then we strive even harder, and we do everything we can to create that résumé that supposedly gives us what we need. But we don't stop to ask ourselves, Am I happy? Am I thriving? *And if not, what on earth do I do?*

This book is a roadmap to finding your own answer to this question. Jennet Ingle—one of the sunniest, most resourceful, and most generous human beings I know—doesn't just hand you a bunch of platitudes. She's been there. She understands the struggle. And she's figured out how to truly thrive as an artist, on her terms.

She walks the walk. And she's inviting you to walk alongside her as you take ownership of your own path to a thriving life as a professional musician.

The Happiest Musician is loaded with practical tools, real talk, and—importantly—with empathy. Jennet Ingle dispenses with the old rules about what a "successful" career has to look like, and she helps paint a picture of what is truly possible—not just for her, but for any of us.

This book is premised on the radical idea that you get to decide what you need, you get to define what success means to you, and you have the tools to make it happen. You hold the vision, you have the power. And you can work to create more happiness in your own life, starting today. No more gatekeepers, no more shame about "not making it," (or about "making it" but not being satisfied). You deserve to thrive, and Jennet Ingle's marvelous book will help you learn how.

Introduction

If you weren't a musician, what would you do for a living? What are the top five careers you could see yourself in? This party game was one my musician friends and I used to love to play, because it was always so deliciously revealing. No matter how seemingly unrelated someone's choices were, we could always find a common thread leading back to their essence.

Here are the rules: skill and training don't matter. The question is not, *What would you pivot to right now for a career change?* But rather, if things had gone differently and you were fully qualified to do something else, what would you want to be?

My five choices: Stand-Up Comic, Figure Skater, Con Artist, Charismatic Preacher, Tennis Star.

I would name the most diverse things I could think of that I knew I'd love, and then I'd analyze my list. Every choice was totally impractical, of course. I wasn't going to be a con artist, because I'm not a crook. I wasn't going to be a revival tent preacher because I'm an atheist. I wasn't going to be a skater or a tennis pro because I have no physical talent for those things.

But these all rhyme with being a Principal Oboe, right? They all have to do with being the best in a very specific niche. They all have to do with doing or making within very close confines. They are all about communication and artistry, but they are also solitary pursuits.

It's very clear what success would look like in these fields, and if I'm successful I alone can take credit for my success; there's not a teamwork component in any of these choices. (I'm not great at team sports, because there's no "I" in "team.")

Disappearing into the fabric of the group does not suit me. Managing people does not interest me. Inspiring people does. Being onstage and making people feel a certain way is what I live for.

I can easily imagine a different version of a musical career that would suit me less well. A musician might tour with a Broadway musical, play the same repertoire every night, always in a supporting role (always the oboist, never the *ingénue*), and never have a connection with the audience or with other musicians outside of the pit.

This gig might pay well, and a person might be happy and fulfilled doing it. But I would get bored and would feel stifled, and would grow to resent the whole structure that kept me from pursuing my own projects.

It turns out that I'm in the perfect field for me, but that's not an accident. I've crafted my career very intentionally to suit me and to provide what I need to thrive.

I do perform as Principal Oboe; within the orchestra it's one of the most soloistic positions. I give concerto performances as often as I can, putting me even further out in front. Since concertos rarely come up more than once or twice a year, I feed that solo addiction with recitals.

Generally, I put together one or two programs a year, and perform them over and over. Every time I perform, I make a point of speaking, to bring the audience along on my journey. I want them to have some idea of how to listen to the piece, and I want them to get to know me.

I have a video channel that I use to educate and entertain other oboists. I have a blog that I use to reach out to the world. I teach in a way that feeds my love of speaking to groups.

YOUR DREAM CAREERS

What are your five dream careers? What would you be doing right now, if you had known at age 10 what you know now?

Let these choices be as wild as you like. Think about the day-to-day work. Make sure you love the idea of doing what you'd be doing.

Now, find the connections. What is it exactly that appeals to you? Do you have that in your life now? Why or why not? Is there a way to bring it in?

There are plenty of different ways to be a musician. You could be an ensemble player or a soloist. A band member or a front-man.

You could focus with laser intensity on one instrument, or be a doubler who can do anything.

You could be a music critic and write about music. You could be a composer, and create it from scratch.

You could be focused on making instruments, or making reeds, or on educating young players. You could improvise or read from printed music.

All of the choices in the world are available to you within the framework of "musician." What do you want to be?

This wealth of choices was not always clear to me. Twenty-five years ago, when I graduated from one of this country's top conservatories, I expected that I would quickly get a job—a *big* job, in an orchestra—the kind of job that would pay me a full time salary with benefits, the kind that would establish me as an important musician, the kind that would give me the credibility to tour with solo recitals and to attract high-level students.

I was taught and trained to believe that this was the goal—the *only* way to be a successful musician.

And I had to be successful.

If I wasn't successful, it would prove that my tenth grade science teacher was right, and that I should have worked harder in science. It would prove that my parents were right and that I should have gotten an education degree as a fallback. It would prove that I wasn't as good as I thought I was, that I was a failure as a human. It would make *me* a failure.

I took auditions for years. Over and over again, I almost won a big job. And then... I didn't. Those years were filled with heartbreak and self-doubt.

Meanwhile, I was creating my actual life every day. I was going to jobs to pay the bills. I was gigging to make bits of money. I was teaching students and then better students. I was giving little performances with my quintet and by myself. I was making reeds for myself, then for a local freelancer, then for the city, and then for everyone.

Eventually, I was playing for my own small orchestras, and getting married, and buying cars and houses, and having a baby, and... And suddenly I realized that I *had* a life, and a career made up of a million little jobs. And I realized that I loved it.

THE HAPPIEST MUSICIAN

I am the happiest musician I know.

I am not objectively the most successful musician I know by any metric. I have not won an audition for a Big Five orchestra. I do not have a tenured professorship at a prestigious university. I am not a household name. I have never held a full-time job. I buy my family's health insurance out of pocket. I do not make tens of thousands of dollars for an appearance, and I do not have my picture on bubble gum cards.

But I do have work that I love and that suits me perfectly. I have an audience that knows me and follows me and responds when I talk to them. I have clients and students that I love and who challenge me in the ways I love most. I have figured out what makes me happy and what I am good at and what I enjoy. By intentionally doing a number of different things that each have their own pacing and their own strategy and their own income stream, I have a stable financial foundation. I am thriving.

I can accept offered work that suits me and that I am excited about. I can turn down work that doesn't. I can create my own work. I can try ideas out and double down on them or pivot to new ones. I'm always looking for new challenges, new experiences, new ways to be a creative person in the world, and I am making good money doing this.

I want this for you, too.

Too many musicians, artists, writers, and creatives have been taught to follow a narrow path to success, to apply to gatekeepers for entry, and to consider themselves lesser if they can't make it past those gates. Too many wait to be chosen and give up when they aren't. Too many are cynical and discouraged, too many talented people choose to quit the profession because they just can't seem to make it work. I'd like you to see that you can claim some agency in your own life and career!

In the following pages, we'll explore the reality of our current musical landscape and look at some of the gifts that brought you into this profession and some of the mindset issues that may be keeping you stuck. I will introduce the Portfolio Career as a way to choose your own creative, artistic, and financial path forward.

I will tell my story and break down the aspects of my work that are keeping me secure, comfortable, and deeply fulfilled. We'll talk about money and how to demystify and simplify it for yourself. I'll help you figure out how you want to structure your career and lifestyle.

This book is the story of an oboist, me. But this is not a book for oboists alone.

I love podcasts, but rarely listen to interviews with musicians. It doesn't feel exciting to me to hear a clarinetist talking about her reeds or practice habits, although I can talk about mine all day. I know too much, and hearing the text of what she says is less interesting than listening hard for subtext in the journey of another creative person.

In contrast, I am thrilled to hear an interview with an actor who talks about his craft, an entrepreneur who breaks down her launch strategy, an author who discusses his process. When I listen to these creative people talk about what they do, my mind makes leaps and connections, and I come up with ideas for my own craft, my own business, my own artistry.

I hope that throughout this book you can see that the paths I've chosen are not exclusive to me. I'll tell my specific story, but I invite you to read between the lines. I'll show you that you can build your own ways to make money as a creative.

I want you to apply these lessons, these ideas, to the artistic path that is right for you. And I want you to find a way to thrive in the world as a musician, or an artist, or a photographer. I want you to bring your magic to the world.

AN INVITATION

When you are living your life, every choice that comes up feels like a completely independent one, one that requires a lot of thinking and agonizing. It is difficult to feel like you have an overview of what is going on. During this writing process, though, I began to see connecting threads, guidelines that have helped me over and over again.

I invite you to look at the ways these snippets of advice might play into your own story, at the ways you might zoom out and think about your own career in a new or different way.

Ask yourself: What do you need to thrive as a creative person? What would you need to be the happiest musician?

1. **Get clear.** Know what you want and what you don't.
2. **Know what you need to thrive.** Not survive but truly thrive.
3. **Let things evolve.** You don't have to burn down the whole place and dramatically pivot. Maybe just try something new and see how it fits!
4. **Be curious.** This is especially powerful when things feel bad. What is the worst part of this? How could it be better?

5. **Create structure.** Nurture small habits and simple routines that keep you moving forward.
6. **Get help.** Whatever you are struggling with, you are not the first person ever to experience it. Someone is out there to give you a hand forward. Google. Ask. You don't have to do everything alone.
7. **Find your people.** Surround yourself with people who support you. Find your tribe. Find your partner. Find your audience.
8. **Just start.** You'll be surprised how much easier things get as soon as you try doing them.

PART ONE
Seeing the Reality

1

A Music Career Is Hard!

During my high school years, I remember at least two occasions when old cranky violinists spoke to groups of optimistic young musicians about *not* going into music. One was a session during a Rochester Philharmonic Youth Orchestra retreat in which an actual RPO professional (who was probably 47, but whom I recall as ancient) told us that statistically no one who graduates from music school wins an audition for a job because there are only, like, four jobs available in the world at any one time and 7,000 young hotshots entering the scene every week.

Quit now!

I may have misremembered the details of this speech, but I distinctly recall the emotional jolt. It was designed to discourage.

Parents, on the whole, do not want their children to go to music school, much less pursue a career in performance. Most of us have heard, "Why don't you at least get an education degree? At least then you could get a job." As you can imagine, I have a lot of thoughts around this kind of preemptive Plan B thinking. I'll share those thoughts with you in *Chapter 8: Creating a Teaching Career.*

We can understand where parents and seasoned professionals are coming from. Classical music is, let's be frank, not a growing field. Even before COVID-19 shut down all performance venues and live events everywhere, arts organizations had long been struggling to stay solvent. It is hard to work in this business and hard to scrape together a decent living.

Why must this be so difficult?

ARTS ORGANIZATIONS ARE BECOMING LESS RELEVANT

Every few years, we see another think piece about how Classical Music is dying. Audiences are aging, the next generation of philanthropists is focusing on other issues, and society doesn't care about the arts. No one seems to want to come to concerts, or so say the doom-mongers.

Every few years, we see another formerly significant arts institution in a struggle to survive. Orchestras have folded in the past few decades in Syracuse, Savannah, Albuquerque, and Honolulu. The Philadelphia Orchestra has declared bankruptcy, the Louisville Symphony did the same, the Minnesota Orchestra locked its musicians out for nearly a year.

Universities are scrambling as well. We've recently seen music departments eliminated and colleges downgrading from tenure-track to adjunct faculty positions across the United States. As I'm writing this, I'm following a story from the University of Evansville in Indiana, where the university is attempting to eliminate the entire music department—all of the performing majors and all of the tenured faculty—people who have established their lives (and livelihoods) in this town.

As the older generation of music lovers and philanthropists begins to opt out of leaving home for concerts and begins to pass on, a new audience with new needs is taking its place.

Many orchestral organizations, many conservatories, and even many musicians are struggling to pivot into an offering that will appeal to this newer generation without pandering or sacrificing the quality of the music they offer.

Some are doing better than others, but across the industry this is a challenge that will not go away.

JOB DISSATISFACTION

Once you get a job—whether a coveted "unicorn" position in a major orchestra or top university or a smaller "anchor" job that just pays the bills—the question of job satisfaction arises.

A famous study from the 1990s found that orchestral musicians have lower job satisfaction than prison guards. And this feels anecdotally correct. I am the happiest musician I know. But it's a pretty low bar.

For the most part, musicians in an orchestra have no artistic control. They are not in charge of musical programming or of the overall direction of the organization. They are led by a conductor whose philosophy and interpretations cannot be challenged. They have no ability to choose their colleagues—the people they sit next to and work closely with day in and day out.

If you don't get along with your stand partner or with the person sitting next to you in your institutionally assigned seat, your options are either to leave the orchestra or to wait for the other person to do so. There's no room for personal choice in this environment.

As an orchestral musician, your job every day is to chase impossible perfection, to pursue ever closer adherence to an "ideal" performance, and above all to not make mistakes. Especially for section players, there's little to no room for individual expression or artistic license—your work is either right or wrong, and if your playing gets too fancy or interesting, it will get noticed and will get you reprimanded.

It is a pleasure to play great orchestral repertoire. But over the long term, a musician's lack of agency within the ensemble can lead to discouragement, cynicism, and *ennui*. At least those great jobs pay well, though, right? Right?

THE MONEY

No one goes into music for the money, or so they say. Still, the money is embarrassingly bad in many cases. Even in those big jobs, the so-called "unicorn" positions, we are not for the most part talking about real wealth.

Yes, some orchestras do pay six-figure salaries. However, those orchestras also tend to be in major cities, where $200,000 doesn't go as far as anyone would like it to.

There's a romantic trope surrounding the "starving artist," a feeling that making real money is "selling out," and that doing "what we love" should be sufficient reward. As artists, these ideas are deeply embedded in our belief systems and social DNA. Even in a symphonic organization with a reasonably savvy board of directors, these factors are leveraged against musicians when it comes to negotiating increases in salary, bonuses, even per diem expenses.

Wait!

Because we love music, because we have chosen to use our considerable talents to make beauty in the world instead of, say, drilling for oil, we should be satisfied with a $6 lunch allowance? Raise your hand if you recently had a healthy, enjoyable meal for $6.

It's not about the money, right? No one goes into the arts to be a millionaire, and if you want to be rich, there are plenty of easier ways to achieve that than a music career. There are jobs that pay real money, there are other career paths where mid-six-figure salaries are the norm.

It would be easy to decide against music if money were the most important factor. This is not for us. We are in music because something about this field stirs us so deeply, calls to us so strongly, that everything else feels like a disappointing fallback.

But money isn't irrelevant. It is an energy, a resource we all need to live. Money makes things easier in our day-to-day lives, and it can transform a life of struggle into a life that feels comfortable and aligned for us and our values. At a minimum, money can make it easier to simply do the things we want to do, to fuel our dreams.

If you won the lottery tomorrow and you had all the money you could ever want, would you quit music? At certain points in my life, I might have said things like:

"No, but I would quit my day job at the bagel shop so I could practice."

"No, I would use it to pay for plane tickets so I never had to miss an audition I wanted to take."

"No, I would use it for a housekeeper so I didn't have to waste my creative time vacuuming my studio."

"No, I would use it to get this chamber music series off the ground and make sure I can pay my colleagues."

"No, I would use it to create a new orchestra in this town that doesn't have one."

In other words, I saw money as a path to a bigger and better music career, not an end in itself.

I know people who are still wishing for that lottery win. People who draw a salary from their music job, and have only that amount of money—the same every week—until the next contract negotiation. People who are making their living freelancing and teaching, but barely, with untold, unpaid hours wasted on the road.

As a freelancer, you are often limited to a yes/no decision on whether to accept offered work at a set rate. When you teach for a school, your wage is usually fixed.

If you teach private students at home, you have quite a bit more flexibility in what you will charge—but that flexibility is not always part of a musician's toolbox. Many allow their rate to be set by the local market instead of doing what is best for them and for their students. So they end up underpaid, overworked, and disappointed in their musical careers.

It doesn't have to be this way!

At this point in my life, I would not even consider playing the lottery. As is true for everyone, small expenses can add up and my family is conscious about silly spending (like the lottery!) but we can comfortably afford to live with the combined income from my teaching and coaching, my reed-making business, and solo and orchestral performances. I don't need more! I am not being modest and humble; rather, I am earning a very comfortable living in music and I feel wealthy enough to not have to seek more.

I want that for you, too!

WHAT DOES SUCCESS MEAN?

If your definition of success is getting a permanent job that will pay your salary and benefits, keep you in the upper middle class, and provide a retirement pension, it is absolutely true that a creative career is not the safest route. These kinds of jobs do exist, but they are vanishingly rare and fiercely difficult to win. Artists in these positions are both extraordinarily talented and exceptionally lucky—and they know it.

Every year, more and more amazing young musicians graduate from school, enter the job market, and hit the audition circuit. The demand for these scarce single-paycheck jobs in music has outpaced supply to an absurd degree.

It's interesting, though, because those big one-paycheck jobs are actually not that secure.

Every three to five years, orchestras' union contracts come up for renegotiation and anything can happen. There might be raises, but there also might be wage freezes, cuts, strikes, or lockouts. There can be bad faith bargaining. Many orchestra management teams can't seem to find ways to stay relevant in their communities.

Orchestras can fold up and die, throwing all of their musicians out of work overnight. These are the musicians who had already "made it," who had hit the big time, and who were enjoying that single-paycheck job. When it goes away, they have no safety net.

This is such a dangerous place to be!

Depending on how long you've been in that job and relying on that paycheck, you might not be in excellent audition shape to go out and win another position in an increasingly competitive climate. You might not be able to slide into another similar job, certainly not in your current city, the one which no longer has an orchestra. You may not be mentally or emotionally prepared for the hustle of being a gigging musician. You might think that you have no training for anything else, you might feel that your life is over.

But keep reading. There is another path.

2

We Make It Harder

In the very first session of my freshman year at the Eastman School of Music, my teacher Richard Killmer posed the question, "Do you have to play the oboe?" My response was unambiguous: Yes!

Everyone has their own reason for wanting to be in this field. Some just love music so much they can't live without it. Some enjoy the craft of the instrument itself, others the camaraderie and the in-the-trenches feeling of pulling together an orchestra concert. Some are natural performers who need to be in front of a crowd. Some revel in their connection to history and the creativity of great minds from before their time.

For me, it's the promise of the *flow state* that I can't walk away from. I'm addicted to the feeling of deep focus I can access when I'm practicing and performing. Music is such an easy way into this state!

Isn't it interesting, though? We all have these clear feelings about why we can't give up our life in music, even though the negative aspects of the profession are clear to all. There's something about the adversity of our early training, about the way we are encouraged to persevere, something about the way young musicians are discouraged out of the professions. By the time we get to, and through, our music degrees, we've had this conversation over and over again with our parents, our teachers, our counselors, and our colleagues. We have dug in, we are stubborn. We have drunk the Kool Aid.

YOU'RE AMAZING!

Musicians are amazing. To get to where they are, they've worked and sacrificed their whole lives. This is probably just as true for you as it was for me—and for virtually all trained musicians.

In middle school and high school, you got teased; yet you continued to practice your instrument and take lessons. You had to make choices at that age. If sports conflicted with band, what would you do? If there wasn't enough money for music lessons *and* new stylish clothes, what would you do?

Somehow, around all the chaos of other adolescents coming of age at the same time, you chose a path that was specialized and difficult, and you proceeded on that path to college, university, or conservatory.

In music school, you learned to work and to work harder. You learned that improvement doesn't happen in lessons, it happens in the practice room—and you showed up every day.

In music school, you learned to be relentlessly self-critical, to ceaselessly strive for better, to listen to others and judge yourself against them.

You learned to compare yourself to recordings, and to the artificial perfection inherent in that medium. You learned that you would never be good enough. You went to the parties, but then you came back to the practice room, because nothing was more important than that work.

As you worked on yourself in your practice room, you also learned to work with others in chamber music and in orchestra. You learned how to acknowledge strengths and gracefully approach weaknesses in others. You learned how to graciously accept feedback, and how to generously deliver it. How to create a compelling interpretation, then how to change it on request. How to fit seamlessly into an ensemble as a supportive team player, and how to step forward and lead when required.

Think about all the skills involved in performing music at a high level. You are amazing!

Musicians know how to take a complex passage or large-scale piece and break the task down into manageable chunks, and then to devise creative strategies to practice and perfect it.

Musicians know how to pay attention to their bodies and how to work through pain, but also how to mindfully modify their physical approach to prevent injuries.

Musicians know how to study and honor the traditions of the past while also allowing their unique personalities to shine through.

They know how to collaborate with others and how to give and accept feedback.

In live concerts, they can deliver high-level performance on their instrument while reacting in real time to input around them. They are present in a way that few people can be.

Musicians are highly skilled, intelligent, and coachable people with a deep work ethic. But they are also trained to strive for an incredibly narrow and limited idea of success.

WHAT IS SUCCESS?

When I graduated from the Eastman School of Music, one of the most revered conservatories in the country, I assumed that I would promptly move into a principal oboe position in a major orchestra and live out my life in regal comfort, playing high-visibility oboe solos and cashing my fancy checks every week. This was the life I expected. Other colleagues had their sights set on tenured professorships at prestigious universities or on prominent solo careers under management.

For most musicians, these three career paths, all rigorously guarded by gatekeepers, are the only traditional markers of success in this industry. If you didn't land one of the big full-time orchestra jobs, if you are still an adjunct professor, or if you are not invited to perform on a big series or stage—then you have not succeeded.

Can we just talk about how limiting that is?

First, there are so few orchestras that actually pay a full-time-with-benefits salary. In most of them, there are no more than three oboe positions—and a player who wins one of these jobs and earns tenure can basically keep it for the rest of their life. They might leave for a different orchestra, or another profession, or retirement. It's ultimately their choice, and inertia is a powerful force. Which means that in a given year, there might be as few as five or six jobs in the United States that actually open up for auditions.

I have been to auditions with as few as 30 candidates, but those auditions are rare. More often, there are 50 to 100 musicians vying for one position. Every one of them paid their own travel expenses, every one of them worked for weeks or months to prepare for this audition, every one of them will be invited to play for ten minutes or less on this stage. And all but one of these passionate and dedicated professionals will walk away without a job. Musicians are conditioned and socialized to understand that this is the path to career success and happiness, and that until they win that one job, they are not allowed to get started in life—much less to find peace, satisfaction, and happiness.

A similar situation is found in academia. Plenty of new DMAs enter the market every year, with not enough tenure-track positions available. And adjunct teaching, I can tell you from experience, is for the birds. No money, no respect, no control.

In general, musicians have been taught to respect this hierarchy. After all, our teachers and mentors came up through this system and they believe in it. The educational system as a whole has not caught up with the realities of the modern job market. Some conservatories may offer a token Entrepreneurship class, or an Arts Administration degree program. But if you ask a random group of young players about their career goals, you will hear a consistent and predictable answer: they expect to get big jobs.

I know musicians who keep competing on the audition circuit for years, mentally discounting all of the actual work they are doing in the world as they strive to be chosen, to have a committee validate their worthiness. I know musicians working in the very same orchestras I am working in who have a chip on their shoulders and an inferiority complex about their place in the hierarchy. Not all of them, of course. But more than a few.

We tend to hold in high esteem those players who have hit the big time—and we should, of course. They have demonstrated the talent and the work ethic and the perseverance to achieve what they have. They are fantastic musicians and wonderful people. They show up on stage night after night and deliver stunning, beautiful work. Playing consistently in those top ensembles keeps their skills honed to a high degree. They are gifted, amazing people, and they know they are lucky to have the positions they have. But—and I am sure they would agree with me here—they are still people. They aren't always satisfied with their own playing, they don't always feel like winners, sometimes they are tired and cranky, they make mistakes, and they are not inherently better humans than you or me. They are people with careers, and so are we.

YOU DON'T HAVE TO WAIT

Think of the number of musicians you personally know. Those who are freelancing at a regional or local level, perceiving themselves as failures. Those who are in mid-level orchestras, wishing they were in big ones, and perceiving themselves as failures. Those who have just graduated and are waiting tables, and perceiving themselves as failures.

There are a lot of talented and highly skilled artists out there who have been taught that winning a big orchestra job (or a big teaching job, etc.) is the only way you get to call yourself a success—and that every version of a career that is not precisely this is not success. These beliefs are deeply embedded through continuous repetition and reinforcement throughout our academic and professional lives.

As musicians live through their 20s and 30s—as their friends and colleagues are advancing in their non-musical careers, having babies, and buying houses—many musicians are waiting. They are preparing for auditions, they are sending resumes, they are working day jobs and regional music gigs, and they are waiting to get that big job before they dare to buy a house, to start a family, or even to date. If the very next audition might uproot you across the country, why bother putting down roots?

Let me say that again, more plainly. According to this messaging, you have to be chosen—selected from a huge pool of talent as one of the top players or teachers in the country—before you can begin to develop your artistry for yourself rather than for an audition committee. You have to be settled in your well-established orchestra or college before you can take your eyes off the ball and even begin thinking about any sort of hobby, any sort of alternate income stream. You have to be affiliated with the one orchestra you will spend the rest of your days with before you can buy a house, find a partner, or have a child.

I talked with a close friend about my dreams, back when she and I were fully engaged in the audition mindset. I said, "I don't mind these little orchestra jobs I have. I just want to be able to give recitals and masterclasses and have orchestras offer me concertos, too. Is that so much to ask?" And she said, "No, that's totally reasonable, but I think it will be so much easier to have those things once you have a big job."

I remember this conversation vividly because I thought about it for years every time I considered whether or not to take an audition. Instead of, "Do I want to move to this town? Do I want this job?" my mental calculus was, "If I want to have the credibility to show up as a performer and teacher, I'd better try for this one."

I was recently in a conversation with an entrepreneurially minded colleague, who named a famous principal player of his instrument, and said, "If he and I both tried to start a program, all the students would flock to him." This is another way to say that unless you have that one job, all other opportunities are closed to you.

That's crazy, right? The world is not just sitting there waiting for that famous player to decide to create a group program, or a touring ensemble, or a teaching studio. He might not even want to do that! He might not have time! Why not do it yourself?

CRAB MENTALITY

You've heard the metaphor of the crabs in the pot? A single crab could easily climb out and escape to safety, but a pot full of crabs will stay in the water and boil to death. Any crab that tries to leave will be pulled back down by the others. They don't realize that they're dooming the whole group to being eaten. They just don't like seeing any one crab doing something different, something outside the box. Or pot.

Many musicians have internalized this way of being. They look askance at artists who try to monetize outside the traditional paths. They believe that musicians in small orchestras are not merely less successful but less valid than their colleagues in big orchestras. They believe that musicians with interests outside of music or with day jobs are not serious about their art. They believe that the desire to make money and live comfortably equates to selling out.

I scorn this concept. I celebrate my colleagues who are creating new ways of being successful in the world, and using their artistry with intention, for themselves. I am a huge proponent of diversification and not waiting for others to define or create success for me.

Yet this same internalized fear rears up each time I have a new idea or launch another offer. What will *they* think of me? Will *they* think I'm not a real musician anymore? It seems so ridiculous, but it's there. The crabs *in my head* are trying desperately to drag me back down.

Many musicians actually believe that they are not qualified for anything other than playing their instruments or teaching others to play. They believe that the path to greater success involves practicing harder and longer and waiting for someone to choose them.

I once believed this. I ran around on the audition circuit for years, and sat on mismatched furniture in tiny apartments, and didn't share my playing or my thoughts with anyone because I didn't yet have a full-time orchestra job. Because I didn't have a big job, I wasn't "allowed" to promote myself as a teacher, as a soloist, as a thought leader. I was waiting.

But the things I thought I needed a big job for turned out to be things I could create for myself. I could have high-level students and help them achieve great things. I could create my own platform for writing. I could give recital performances. I could commission new works. I could make my own money. I didn't have to be more "established" as an oboist; I only had to be willing to do the things I was good at and to help other people do the same.

Imagine a world in which musicians respected and appreciated themselves and each other. What if they allowed the world to see them as multi-faceted human beings with a range of valuable talents and strengths? What if those 10,000 hours of focused and self-directed work actually translated to the real world as a superpower?

Imagine a world in which musicians realized that they were allowed to *choose themselves!* When I saw that I did not have to wait for the approval of my industry and that I could choose myself, I understood that what I had was a portfolio career.

3

The Portfolio Career

Let's talk about what success could look like if it didn't have to be built around one big-name job. Let's talk about what it might look like to control your own schedule, your own mix of projects and opportunities that delight you, and to be able to evolve as you go along.

What if, instead of one fixed paycheck that looks the same every week and into which you have to fit your expanding grown-up life, you had multiple income streams, multiple creative outlets, multiple possibilities, and you were solely in charge of how you wanted to keep them in balance? What if you *could* do more than one thing and do it well? Because you can. What if you were allowed to? Because you are.

For past generations, especially here in the United States where a full-time job was the only guaranteed way to procure health insurance, winning that single position became the main goal, the main mark of a grownup. You'd look at the actor/waiter or the bartender/screenwriter with pity, as someone who might never make it in the real world, someone who just hadn't yet come to grips with reality.

We don't have to be limited by that way of thinking anymore! To have multiple interests is a mark of creativity; to have a level of security from a job you enjoy is smart. If I had to put a label on my own career, I'd say I'm a musician/entrepreneur/teacher/writer/coach, and I wear those slashes with great pride, because I've developed all of those roles myself.

In his 1994 book, *The Empty Raincoat,* Charles Handy introduced the concept of a Portfolio Career, one which is made up of an intentional mix of jobs and projects and income streams. The success I've achieved has come from putting together a large number of tiny jobs—regional orchestra positions, sub and extra musician gigs, solo performances, adjunct teaching jobs—with a private teaching studio and other entrepreneurial projects I've created for myself.

I have greater job security than many of my colleagues in more prestigious positions, because any one or two jobs could fold up and disappear without affecting my bottom line. I can create a new offer, take on a new student or client, seek another opportunity to take its place. And I can make choices that feel good and right to me rather than having to show up for work that doesn't spark joy.

The "gig economy" has gotten a bad rap lately, with Uber drivers and Task Rabbits and Fiverr contractors all struggling to make ends meet. Our capitalist society is surging with startups trying to find ever more efficient ways to take advantage of people. In some ways, a portfolio career can look like embracing that gig economy, but the distinction lies in having a vision for what that career might look like, creating it intentionally instead of allowing yourself to mark time in a gig-type job that isn't moving you forward either in terms of your bottom line or your artistry.

I propose that the portfolio career can be more secure, more flexible, more fulfilling, and even more lucrative than any of the traditional musician success paths we have been raised to believe in. I would like to advocate for musicians and artists taking agency in their lives, including choosing where to live, how to balance their interests, who to work with, and what to charge. I would like to offer the idea that success might not come exclusively from having won a Unicorn Position, but from creating a life filled with activities you love to do that pay enough to live comfortably, whatever that means for you.

If you can begin to think about your career in terms of multiple income streams, rather than focusing on being chosen for any one job; if you can let that church gig and that side hustle and that recital idea and that orchestra week and those five students all collectively *be* the point, instead of a distraction *from* the point; you might begin to *see* that point differently.

When my main project was taking auditions, but I still had to live, I had a day job selling tickets and a side hustle selling reeds and a principal oboe job far away from my home, plus local gigs from time to time. All of those things were going just fine, and combining to support me sufficiently in my low-budget 20s. But I wonder how much faster I could have evolved if I'd thought to lean in and intentionally develop those multiple streams as growth opportunities.

In 2008, when global financial crises piled up one after the other and banks were bailed out because they were "too big to fail," my husband (also a freelance musician) and I tightened our belts and joked that we were "too small to fail." A summer festival we had long loved went under; oh well, that gave me another week to teach in the summer. A reed subscriber quit; another one took her place. Orchestral contract negotiations cut my pay; another college brought me on as an adjunct. Our income was so diversified that we had a tremendous amount of security. No one financial hit could sink us.

In 2020, even when COVID-19 struck and eliminated all orchestral performances and 30% of my reed business, I had enough alternate income streams to survive in addition to the business foundation, adaptability, and support to create more streams as needed. We continue to live through this extended pandemic comfortably. Some of my colleagues with unicorn jobs have not been as fortunate.

The COVID pandemic is an extreme case, right? But there are always surprises. Even in normal times, you'll sometimes have a few students quit suddenly. Or a labor negotiation that goes sideways and cuts concerts from your season. Or an unexpected car repair, or a medical bill. Things just happen sometimes, and when you are on a fixed income it can be hard to roll with the punches. If you are actively nurturing a variety of income streams, you will find that it's relatively easy to be resilient, and that the money always seems to come from somewhere.

TAKE THE PRESSURE OFF YOUR ARTISTRY

When my husband Steve and I were getting started, our goal was to make our living exclusively from music. We wanted to be performers, maybe teachers, even reed-makers—but certainly *not* dog walkers or ticket sellers or bagel sandwich makers. It wasn't immediate, but within a few years we had achieved that goal. We didn't have to work behind a counter forever.

Today, I look back on that attitude and ask myself: What would have been so bad about keeping those jobs, or some sort of job, if I enjoyed it?

It felt like a huge point of pride for me to quit and stay home to make reeds, but in retrospect that's a lot of pressure to put on the oboe, which suddenly had to be my entire life. I loved it and I was happy—but that choice might not be right for you. If you are working a day job beside your music, if you are enjoying it, if it is providing purpose and social structure and *flow* in your life—it's OK for that to be a part of your portfolio career!

Being able to comfortably pay your rent every month does not make you less of an artist.

My favorite non-music job was working in a Hess gas station after my freshman year of college. I had plenty of jobs before and after that—I worked in libraries, I made bagel sandwiches, I was in ticket sales and patron services, and one summer I dug up and reset bricks in a lady's yard—but working at the Hess Mart was satisfyingly sociable, low-stakes, and easy, and I loved sorting and counting the boxes of cigarettes and drinking the burned coffee and daydreaming between customers.

The money was terrible but I was living with my parents and didn't really care. The job gave structure to my days but didn't burn out my creativity or physical energy, so I could be devoted to my own projects the rest of the time. Minimum wage work is not a path I recommend, but having a job that demands little of you so you can be fresh for your art can be a beautiful thing. On the other hand, having a job that *does* challenge you, *does* delight you, *does* spark your creative juices and remunerates you well is fantastic!

I have colleagues with full time non-music positions who still make time to practice and play at a high level. They sometimes have to turn down playing work that falls during the day, but life is full of choices, and they find that their artistry is a joyful outlet for them. The gigs they can't accept don't hurt their bottom line; the "day job" takes care of that. And they are beautiful players, and serious musicians, who have created a balance that works for them.

Your instrument doesn't have to be your complete identity as a human being; your musical artistry doesn't have to support your life entirely. You are more than your instrument.

MAKE YOUR OWN CHOICES

A portfolio career empowers you to create your own path. If you are not in a full-time job working for someone else, then you are allowed to make your days, weeks, and months look like you want them to. It may not be possible to snap your fingers and—*Poof!*—have your dream life fully fleshed out. But it is certainly possible to evolve toward any version of balance you can imagine.

You can make choices about the projects you want to create—the CDs, books, performances, tours, festivals—and you can choose which ones to pursue now and which to pursue later. You can take into consideration who you want on your team; you can work with colleagues who will support you, or who will inspire you, or who are the easiest people to get along with.

You can make choices about your clients or your students. When you teach through a school or a store, you have to accept whoever comes in through the door. If you establish your own private studio, though, you can be more selective. You can choose to work with an age group that suits your style, and you can select the strongest students or the ones who need the most help. You can prioritize group sessions or individual lessons. COVID has made online learning possible for everyone. Do you want to focus on the people living in your local area, or people across the globe? You can teach just the basics of your instrument, or you can specialize in audition preparation, reed making, body mapping, or stage presence.

When it is your thing, you can decide how you want it to look *and* how you want to show up!

Are you good at leading groups? Do you prefer to work one-to-one? Do you like the thought of pre-recording your content so that you can control every aspect of its presentation? Or is it better for you to deliver your message live? Do you want to create in-person experiences? Or stay at home behind your computer screen? Do you want to write, or speak, or just play your instrument? When you think about reaching out to new clients or students or potential collaborators, what version of that feels easy and fun to deliver?

The best part? You can try things out and make changes as you go.

The ideal number of one-to-one students for me in a given week is not zero, and it's not twenty. I've tried both versions, so I know. I currently work with two to three groups in a week and have four or five individual sessions, and every week feels a little different, which for me is amazing. I enjoy being busy every day, but I also need downtime and am still exploring what my best schedule might look like.

The right number of orchestra services for me in a given week is not zero, and it's not more than eight or so. The most comfortable distance for me to commute is not three miles each way—that's too fast, and I don't have time to mentally transition. But less than 60 miles is optimal so I don't waste my whole day driving.

See how this works? Because I have enough things going on that the money always comes from somewhere, I can be selective around new offers that come my way, and increasingly I can have it the way I like it.

UNCAP YOUR INCOME

With a portfolio career, *you* can take control of how much money you earn.

A given orchestra gig pays what it pays. Your day job pays what it pays. If you teach for a school, you have the salary you negotiate, not more. But if you are working for yourself—in coaching, or teaching, or creating programs, or selling products—you can set your own price.

This gives you an enormous amount of control. You can decide whether your teaching is worth $50 or $200 an hour. You can set the ticket prices for your performances. You can sell your reeds for $18 or for $30. You get to choose.

Sure, pricing is a conversation with your audience. If you want to charge more, you have to find a way to position your offer differently, and you have to convince people that the additional value you bring is worth paying for. That's marketing. There are hundreds of books about it, and it's essential for "pure" musicians as well as for entrepreneurs. But there is something so liberating about knowing that you get to decide how you work and what you charge. It opens the door to so many possibilities.

When you work for someone else, there is an income cap. When you have the freedom to set your own prices for your work and to accept or reject outside offers, that cap disappears.

In my earlier teaching I brought 200% to every oboe lesson, even when I was making $37 per student. I didn't hold back, but I did end my days feeling exhausted and depleted, and I couldn't slow down or take fewer students because there wasn't enough money if I stopped.

Now that I'm working differently, now that I offer high ticket packages instead of hourly lessons, I can over-deliver freely, like I love to do. The exchange feels equal now.

But life is not only about money, of course!

EVOLVE AS AN ARTIST

When you are managing your own portfolio career, you get to choose. It used to be the case that orchestral performing was challenging enough for me. That getting through my gigs without embarrassing myself took all the energy I had.

Playing the oboe is hard! I embraced my relatively mindless job selling tickets because it allowed me to save my energy to practice and perform. And I was happy and fulfilled doing that.

Until I wasn't.

Most musicians don't sweat and practice daily throughout their high school, college, and early professional years because they want to be great at their instrument. I mean, of course they want that—but arriving at that end goal is not the part that is fun.

At heart, musicians enjoy the work, the journey, the ongoing effort to get better and better, the search for that elusive ideal of excellence.

No one spends hours a day, every day, for twenty years, seeking mastery, only to be satisfied when they finally achieve it. It's not actually something you achieve, even, because of course there's always a way to be better, or to imagine being better. That search for greatness is where the joy lies.

But at a certain point it's not hard to be great enough to show up for work every day. The level of artistry, control, excellence, and competitiveness required to get an orchestra job or a professorship is enormous. But most of your days as a professional don't require that kind of intensity. As you settle into the routine of your everyday teaching, rehearsing, and showing up, you can really miss that energy of struggling to attain. You can miss the adrenaline of always striving to improve. When it's easy to be good enough to play Beethoven's 5th again, mastery can start to feel... boring.

This is when some musicians start to get cynical, jaded, and grumpy, while other musicians start to seek new challenges.

This was certainly true for me—once it was no longer scary to go to work, once I was relatively confident in my skills. (The oboe is always out to get you, of course, but my lion-tamer tricks succeed now more often than not).

I got restless. I poured more energy into the reed-making business that I was already running on the side, and grew it to a six-figure enterprise. I created my blog, *Prone Oboe,* and worked at the craft of writing and at the challenge of being personally visible and vulnerable online.

I started other projects—an in-person summer Oboe Reed Boot Camp, a chamber music series, a YouTube channel, a social media page on which I shared my writings about the Tarot (with an associated micro-business doing private readings), and an email newsletter. I produced a CD. I toured several recitals each year. I tried to write poetry, and even briefly took up archery. Not all of these projects were fully successful, but the continuous learning and building kept me interested and happy. I was always working on something that challenged me and kept me in my *flow* state.

And all of these activities ran alongside my orchestra jobs.

Sometimes it felt like a lot of work to keep up the pace I set for myself—a number of obligations would converge at once and I would feel like a juggler frantically trying to keep all of my balls in the air. But that amount of work and risk and energy and creativity felt fun, and kept me excited and enjoying my life.

For you, maybe it's not writing, teaching, video creation, archery, or the Tarot. But most musicians that I know love a challenge.

If mastering the viola, say, is no longer a daily struggle, a violist might bake, or garden, or write, or make jewelry. It's exciting to learn a different craft, to explore creativity in a different way, and to find that flow state when your instrument doesn't give it to you as much anymore. If you can monetize the work that feels fun and interesting to you, you can develop it as another income stream. This can provide stability when the work slows down, and can keep you learning, engaged, and alive!

Maybe you're not sure how to monetize that thing, or whether you even want to. That's fine, of course. I think the crucial ingredient is nurturing that interest in the first place. I do love monetizing things and making money, but if you have an outlet beyond your instrument, or at least beyond your job, that's a big step toward becoming the happiest musician.

The advantage of a portfolio career—one that is intentionally made up of smaller projects—is that you can feel out what you want to do, then try things on for size without getting locked in. Later in this book, you'll read about my "failures"—things I've tried out and not taken forward, at least not in the form in which they began. Every one of them was within my control to start and within my control to stop, which feels both comforting and rewarding. Unlike enrolling in a college or working in a corporation that proves to be the wrong fit, there is no sunk cost in taking on a few students or clients, or in selling something you made. You can start anything and then decide to do it more, less, or not at all. I love the freedom of trying new things now, knowing that I have a stable platform from which to experiment.

I came out of college with a degree in oboe performance. Now I have designed a career I love, which includes performing on the oboe, in and in front of orchestras, and in solo and chamber music recitals. But I also teach, write, create videos, make and sell oboe reeds and supplies, coach groups and individuals, and read Tarot cards. Everything I do is fun for me, and the money always comes from somewhere.

In the next several chapters, I'll show you how I created aspects of my own portfolio career. I'll pull out lessons you can learn from each. But the key message for you to retain is that you can do what you want. You can make your career rewarding in every way—one that you enjoy and cherish, and one that sustains and supports you financially!

NOW YOU TRY

If no one job defines you, you get to define you. In the absence of a boss or conductor constantly telling you exactly what to do and how to do it, *you* get to decide how you want your life to feel.

To have a life that you love as much as I love mine, you do not have to have a reed business and a blog and a video channel and an active social media life and a recital habit and two principal oboe jobs and a dog and two cats and a child and a camper.

But maybe it's worth thinking about what *would* be a part of a life that you love as much as I love mine. We'll dig into this more in Part Three. For now, as you go through your days, just notice.

What brings you the most joy? What activities drain your energy the most? When do you most often find yourself in flow? Where is the money coming from?

Even now, today, you can start leaning into the parts of your life that are working for you, and leaning away from the parts that aren't.

GET CLEAR

Here's a journaling activity for you. Make a list of your current money-making activities, and draw emojis beside them. How much do you love them? How much do you want to quit them?

If you are working a non-music job, congratulations! It's great that you are taking care of your financial needs. Do you like it? How is the money compared to the time and energy it costs you? Would it feel good to advance in this job in some way, getting better and better at it? Would it feel better to reduce your hours or to treat it as a convenient distraction from your own big personal project? What's good and bad about this job?

In what ways are you working in music? Do you want more work like that? How might you go about making more connections and getting more and better work?

Are you teaching currently? Could you invite more students, raise your prices, combine them into groups? Are there specific types of students you love or students you don't want to work with anymore?

What else do you enjoy? What other skills might you cultivate? What other strengths do you have? What other hobbies do you love? How might you intentionally allow more things you love to be part of your life?

GET CURIOUS

What would 5% better look like, right now, in any one aspect of your current portfolio?

The thing that's magical about this lifestyle, compared to a permanent salaried job, is how flexible it is! If you are having fun doing what you are doing, you can try to do more of it, or earn more doing it, or tweak it just a bit to make it easier for you to have your very best life. If the work you are doing starts to feel like a grind, you can pivot into something new. Once you figure out how to manage your systems and time, once you develop your talent for monetizing your passions, you get to choose!

SPOTLIGHT ON A CAREER

SHAWNA LAKE

Shawna Lake is the president and creator of Oboe Chicago, and an oboe specialist. Her finest skill set is in helping professional oboists and oboe enthusiasts of all ages listen and find the oboe that fits their "voice," so that oboe, reed, and oboist perform as one.

SHAWNA, HOW WOULD YOU DESCRIBE YOUR CURRENT WORK?

Entrepreneur, professional oboist/performer, and private oboe instructor.

HOW DID YOU START DOING WHAT YOU DO?

In the green room of a recording session, I met a woman who encouraged me and guided me as to how to open my own business and sell oboes.

The next few months were filled with creating a business name, creating a logo with help of a graphic designer, registering with the state of Illinois, doing research to figure out what kind of oboes I wanted to sell and determine why; establish finances for the purpose of buying oboes and proceed to begin putting my face out to people and introduce myself in this capacity and title.

I traveled to the 2006 International Double Reed Society Conference in Muncie, Indiana. I shook hands with and introduced myself to the manufacturers of the oboes I wanted to sell. My business grew quickly and took off with a recognition of need and demand.

WHAT DO YOU LOVE ABOUT YOUR WORK?

I love the variety. Playing oboes, analyzing different kinds of oboes, selling oboes, teaching the oboe to passionate people. I find the magic of helping someone pick and choose a new oboe is *always* special.

WHAT IS THE MOST CHALLENGING ASPECT OF IT FOR YOU?

The most challenging part of what I do is truly making sure to stay on top of my own reed-making and practicing every day. As long as I keep my own skills finely tuned, I am equipped to provide advice and mentor this process of each individual to find their new oboe.

WHAT BARRIERS DID YOU HAVE TO OVERCOME TO GET TO WHERE YOU ARE?

The toughest barrier for me in this business was for me to follow all policies and guidelines I have set up for the business. Not everyone is "my client." My business style and process has been carefully planned to be "in line" with what other companies are doing.

However, not everyone will choose to come to me to buy an oboe. I won't please everyone. This fact is important to remember. In this experience, I found myself growing personally and emotionally.

WHAT ADVICE WOULD YOU GIVE TO SOMEONE WHO WANTED A CAREER LIKE YOURS?

Be sure to ask for help when you need it, and accept advice from professionals you trust. Do research before you plunge in. Be sure to *really* know what you're talking about. Keep your own personal skill set up to date.

IS THERE ANYTHING YOU'D LIKE TO ADD?

A professional music career has many definitions. Create your own definition.

PART TWO
Seeing the Possibility

In Part Two, I'll talk about how I created each of the elements of the life I lead now.

Without even knowing it, I was developing my portfolio career as I went along. Every choice I made was another brick in the foundation. Every time I leaned into a new project I was building my skills and my understanding.

Success is not a linear path.

I tell each thread of my story independently in this book—because it's easier to follow one thread than the day-to-day false starts and dead ends and bill-pay cycles of an actual life, which don't make for great storytelling.

As you read these chapters, you'll see that they have in common a gradually increasing intentionality. I was doing lots of things, and then I began to actually *think* about the things I was doing.

For a long time, I was fully committed to pursuing a major orchestra job, and all of the other bits and pieces of my busy life felt like distractions from that one main goal, or just ways to put food on the table while I waited for success to find me.

My own path was one of constant evolution, but if you think about it, evolution doesn't always move you in the direction you want! Some moves are lateral moves, some are backward. If you don't have 70 million years to experiment with, it's better to be on that path on purpose. Once I realized what I was doing, I was able to set goals, aim intentionally toward them, and achieve them.

In the "Now You Try" sections, I'll talk about ways I would create these elements faster today if I were starting out, taking better, more direct routes. And I'll offer some ways for you to think about your own goals and paths.

The stories here in Part Two are specific to me, but I invite you to read between the lines and take the time to zoom out and consider what your version of such a path might include. Once you get clear on what you really want, you can strategize a way forward.

4

Auditioning

As a part of your portfolio career, you presumably want to do some performing, some *doing* of your craft. You probably didn't make it all the way through music school just to drop your instrument and start teaching and tutoring kids. For most musicians, getting steady playing work is the whole point. Let's talk about how you can make this a reality.

MY AUDITION STORY

When I went to my very first audition I was still in school. I prepared in stealth; I did not tell anyone that I was going to the audition. Why? I think it's that I didn't dare to tell anyone that I had ambitions. Which is nonsense, right? I was at a music conservatory, why wouldn't I start taking auditions? It's that mindset piece again: it has to be perfect, I have to be perfect, and if they knew I was going, they'd see if I failed.

I think my teacher was surprised when I announced that I was going, and we worked on reeds that day as I had nothing great on hand. He gave me one of his as I was leaving—a good-luck gift.

As I pulled into the small Pennsylvania town for that audition, I began to imagine my life as the Principal Oboist of that orchestra. The town was... depressed. Unwelcoming. The audition was held in a church basement. But still, I could imagine myself driving down there from Eastman. I could imagine myself playing solos and starting my professional journey. I could imagine the approbation, the applause.

At the audition, I did not use my teacher's excellent reed. I used a reed I had made, even though it was not as good as his. I had an unjustified pride in my independence. It felt to me as though I would be winning under false pretenses if I played a reed I hadn't made.

I was not in a position to win anyway, right? It was my first time, I was not well prepared, and I didn't really have a sense of what it took to do well at a professional audition. But in my mind, I was a contender, and I was not going to accept charity on my way to my victory.

I was unexpectedly nervous on the stage. It's not that I knew the repertoire inside out, as I do now, but I certainly had practiced it, and I could play it in the privacy of my room. On stage, though, I found my breath coming too quickly, my heart beating too hard. I couldn't do the things I should have been able to do. The blankness of the screen and the silence of the hall felt threatening.

Could I have won this small job on raw talent if I hadn't been so disconcerted by the process? Maybe. I was green but I was a good player. I could have done the job.

Orchestral auditions are their own unique challenge. The task is being able to leap from one style—one acoustical world—to another, playing only the most difficult bits of your repertoire, one after the other. The skill is being able to create a musical context for yourself where none exists in the space around you. In a preliminary round, the job is perfection. Creating this kind of perfection through your physical fear response is something that requires tons of practice—practice I hadn't put in.

I was dismissed after the preliminary round, and I was devastated. Somehow, it felt intensely terrible to lose an audition I was so ambivalent about. If I had been auditioning in a city I was thrilled to be in, if I had been excited about the job, I would have known not to expect to win. But I viewed that small town with scorn and thought I was better than it was—and then I didn't even have the chance to turn it down. They rejected me first. I know this is ridiculous, but it's true. And I've come to realize that it's very human.

This initial rough experience lit a fire in me, though. I became excited and intrigued about the game of auditioning—the game of creating miniature worlds of sound around each excerpt, the game of working through and around my own nervous responses, the game of competing.

For the next fifteen years, I devoted myself to this game.

I read mindset books. I practiced and practiced. I did mock auditions for my friends and colleagues. I listened to other people's mocks. I took as many auditions as I could afford to travel to. I made semis, I made finals, I was runner-up, I lost in the prelim round—over and over and over again. Along the way I won a few jobs (among these are some of the ones I'm still playing today) but the big job, that traditional marker of success, continued to elude me.

Meanwhile, of course, Steve and I were working in Chicago more and more. We'd get the occasional very good gig, and plenty of regional jobs: one to two hours in any direction, with varying degrees of quality and paycheck. We were living small, we were living hand-to-mouth. But all of our activities combined to make us a living, and we were making our living in music!

Years after leaving school, though, I still didn't have that one job that would make me feel validated. I was making my living, sure, but it didn't seem real or grown up. I was still in the musician mind-set, and I knew I hadn't properly made it yet to success.

Then, one evening, I remember trudging into a concert. It was a pops gig, in a bad hall, and I was not enthusiastic about it. It was late spring, or early fall, still light outside as I approached the stage door. I saw the principal trumpet approaching. We waved and greeted each other by name.

Suddenly, I zoomed out of my body as if I were dreaming. I saw the scene as an observer might. And I realized that this was the dream, the one I'd had since I was a kid. I wanted to be the principal oboist of an orchestra. I wanted to be on a collegial first name basis with the other musicians. I wanted to show up to work wearing concert black, and not be anxious or nervous about doing it because it was my job.

And there I was, doing exactly that!

As wonderful as this feeling was, it didn't magically transform the lame pops concert or the problematic management team or the marketing problems that the orchestra had. It didn't change the fact that some of my colleagues annoyed me a little. It did make me realize, however, that sometimes work is work, but that I was, in fact, living my dream.

And I was happy.

Not every concert has to be a milestone. Not every concert has to be fully artistically satisfying. But there I was, being a professional musician. I hadn't taken the most direct or fastest route. It wasn't that arrival moment I had imagined. But that was the moment I realized I was for real.

As I was working through these experiences—waiting and pinning my hopes over and over again on being chosen, on finally breaking through, on finally being validated, and having those hopes dashed time after time—I was still a working musician, freelancing and playing in my own orchestras, and it became increasingly clear what I actually wanted. Not *any* job, but the *right* job.

The right job for me was a principal oboe job in a happy orchestra in a town I liked, with high-level colleagues who challenged me to be better—a job that paid me enough that I could prioritize my time there.

This meant that I didn't actually want a second oboe job even in a Big Five orchestra. It meant that I didn't want to move to Florida for any reason. It meant that an orchestra that rehearses in a basement and performs in a high school auditorium wasn't going to be my end goal.

I don't mind taking gigs like that here and there, but I came to realize that I was willing to make less money to avoid being trapped in an unchanging situation that wasn't the right orchestra job for me.

I thought I wanted a major orchestra position at all costs, but over time it became clear that the things I thought I could get from that major orchestra position were things I could create for myself.

I wanted income stability. I wanted colleagues I loved to work with. I wanted name recognition within my community. I wanted a platform from which to perform concertos and solo recitals. I wanted excellent students. I wanted credibility.

In the 21st century, you don't need a single full-time employer to give you these things.

When I won my current principal oboe job with the South Bend Symphony, it felt clear that this was the one. It wasn't perfect. (Is anything ever perfect?) But the orchestra had a substantial season. It was well-managed. The contract was a serious document, so the job felt serious.

My colleagues in the wind section were and are fantastic, and make me want to live up to their standard and be better. And South Bend is a town that feels homey. It's an inexpensive place to live. It's a liberal community despite being in a conservative state. The people are nice, the colleges are beautiful. I can run along the river every day.

The vision I developed for myself as I was taking auditions in Rust Belt cities and exploring downtowns and grimy backstage areas has very much come together here. My orchestra does not pay a full-time wage. I need the other parts of my portfolio career to help carry the load. But this orchestra gives me what I need emotionally and artistically, and I have the other elements covered in other ways!

I LOVE AUDITIONS

I know I'm ragging on auditions—but I *love* auditions. This may be an unpopular opinion. But I started to have a lot more fun auditioning when I began to treat it as an artistically fulfilling activity, something that could inspire greatness, instead of as something I was likely to fail at.

First of all, I like the game: 50 people come to a hall, one leaves victorious. The drama is deeply satisfying.

I love playing auditions. Picture it: You walk out onto an unfamiliar but beautiful stage, the home stage of an orchestra better than yours. You have the entire space to yourself.

Gazing up into the rows of darkened seats, you can take deep breaths and choose the perfect moment in which to break the silence. You can stand there for up to fifteen minutes, playing all of the best and most famous solos for your instrument to an audience that is listening intently and wanting you to succeed.

You can take these solos at the tempo you choose, with the interpretation you like. No conductor is trying to alter your vision of the piece. It's all about you.

I love sitting behind the screen, too. It's fascinating to listen to other people audition, and to hear what their preparation has brought to the table. Humans are amazing, right? I love watching the Olympics for the same reason: the divers, figure skaters, gymnasts, ski jumpers, etc., are artists as well as athletes.

Although I know nothing of these sports, I find that I can quickly learn to discriminate between the ones who are merely good and the ones who are astounding. It quickly becomes clear what skills are difficult, and what separates the winners from the losers.

In an audition context, even when it's not *my* instrument being auditioned, I rapidly develop a sense of what skills are difficult for the players involved. Once it's clear what I'm listening for, I can sit back and root for them all.

It's interesting to notice how people choose to compensate for the difficulties. It's fascinating to identify the qualities that make me sit up and take notice.

If a candidate comes in and begins immediately to make music—to do something intentional and beautiful and controlled—I'm instantly on their side. I'm hoping they get through the tricky passages; I'm wanting them to succeed.

Honestly, I want everyone to succeed. But once someone grabs my attention by doing something beautiful, I'm all in for them. All I want is to hear great playing—and every ten minutes there's a new person filled with new potential. This is what makes it fun to sit on a committee.

For my own playing, I draw inspiration from the best players I hear. What is it that makes the difference? Did you hear that *perfect* slur up to that high note? I bet I could do something like that!

It's even inspiring to notice what keeps some competitors out of the running. Very often it's not about mistakes that happen in their lists, but simply a lack of attention to detail. Sometimes, particular slurs are sloppy, or articulations don't quite sound clean, or phrases aren't perfectly cared for. The playing is fine, but not great.

I love hearing these reminders to take care of my own house, to make sure that even in my day-to-day playing I am vigilant about the small *sloppinesses* that can creep up, that I remain unimpeachable even in my basic, non-audition work.

I love auditions; I love everything about them.

What if you, too, tried to reframe them as beautiful opportunities to improve and perfect your skills? What if you let this stage of your career be fun and deeply fulfilling? What if, instead of a means to an end, you let an audition be a culminating performance that shows you how beautifully your preparation is progressing?

NOW YOU TRY

Winning auditions is by no means the only way to have a playing career, as you will read in the next several chapters. But if your musical ambitions call you toward orchestral performance, you may want to explore this genre and this skill set. Here are some thoughts.

GET CLEAR ABOUT WHAT YOU WANT

Let's take a moment here to look at your ambitions. When you think about your dream job, what is it that you want? What is the part of it that really excites you? Is it the place? The paycheck? Is it the music-making? Is it the fame? Extra opportunities the position might provide?

Be specific. What kind of position do you want? Do you want to lead or to play in the section? What kind of job would scratch the itch you have? Is there only one way to get there?

CREATE A STRUCTURE FOR YOUR AUDITION WORK

Choose your auditions wisely. There's a time to take some auditions just for practice, but once you see how they work, get focused. Don't spend money to go to auditions you can't win or wouldn't want to win.

FIND YOUR PEOPLE

Surround yourself with people who have similar ambitions. Colleagues and peers will help you prepare. They'll listen to your mock auditions and give you a basis for comparison. They'll motivate you when things are looking bleak.

GET HELP

There are a number of successful musicians offering audition coaching. This is a great idea! Auditioning is a separate skill from simply playing your instrument. It helps to have outside support and advice.

• • •

As you think about your audition journey, though, think about the goal you are trying to achieve. What would the next step in that journey make possible for you? While you are working on that next step, might you also look for another way to achieve that possibility?

Take a moment here and zoom out. While you are taking auditions, could you also be hedging your bets by crafting a freelance network, a teaching studio, a portfolio career that sustains you? You can start now!

SPOTLIGHT ON A CAREER

ROB KNOPPER

Rob Knopper is a percussionist in the Metropolitan Opera Orchestra and founder of *auditionhacker,* an online school that helps keen and motivated orchestra-track musicians achieve their dream career.

ROB, HOW WOULD YOU DESCRIBE YOUR CURRENT WORK?

I'm an opera percussionist and an audition coach.

HOW DID YOU START DOING WHAT YOU DO?

I started how every drummer starts: by banging my hands on the dashboard of our car growing up. Eventually, I started playing drumset and joined as many rock bands as would take me.

I switched to classical in high school when I didn't get into a summer festival for drumset. That got me interested in orchestral percussion and I became fascinated with the idea that there was a fair way—auditions—to win a job with an orchestra that would provide a stable life. After 54 auditions, I won my audition at the Met in 2011.

Getting rejected from most of those 54 auditions made me want to help other orchestral musicians on the same path. I started teaching my techniques for audition preparation which turned into *auditionhacker.*

WHAT DO YOU LOVE ABOUT YOUR WORK?

I love helping people overcome struggles and find success! It is so awesome when a student has a major breakthrough using a practice technique that we worked on together. Seeing my students get to finals, win jobs, and accomplish their goals is incredibly fulfilling.

WHAT'S THE MOST CHALLENGING ASPECT OF IT FOR YOU?

The most challenging aspect of my *auditionhacker* work is trying to achieve the same standard I have for my percussion playing in all of the things I'm trying to do online. I'm never going to match my percussion level when doing things like video editing, writing blogs, storytelling, etc. I will always feel some sort of mediocrity in those areas because I haven't been doing it all my life as I have with percussion. But that certainly doesn't stop me from doing it anyway.

WHAT BARRIERS DID YOU HAVE TO OVERCOME TO GET TO WHERE YOU ARE?

Being open about my failures was a big obstacle for me at first. When I started doing my *auditionhacker* work, there wasn't really anybody online talking about their negative experiences and the audition rejections that they went through. I think it's incredibly important for students to know that getting rejected and experiencing imposter syndrome are totally normal parts of the journey.

WHAT ADVICE WOULD YOU GIVE TO SOMEONE WHO WANTED TO HAVE A CAREER LIKE YOURS?

If you're interested in doing any sort of online coaching or teaching, remember who you are doing it for. Students all over the world can benefit from your work. You may feel that there's an expectation to go in a certain direction because of classical music culture being rooted in a lot of traditions. But remember who you are doing it for and it'll help guide you to building something new.

5

Creating a Freelance Career

I was lucky that when I moved to Chicago I had my Civic Orchestra position to get started with. That job did not pay a lot, but it gave me a place to play right away and a bit of credibility. Still, it took years to develop a network of freelance work that was sufficient to really keep me busy and paid.

Freelancing, though, is the fastest way to start working in a given place, and if I were to move now to a new city, I'd want to get into the scene as quickly as I could.

Every orchestra has its roster of contracted musicians who play every concert, except when they are busy, sick, on vacation, etc. Smaller orchestras often share a pool of musicians. When concert weeks overlap, many players have to make choices. This leaves openings for freelance musicians in town.

Sometimes, an orchestra will program a piece larger than their own players can staff. This creates an opportunity as well. You might find churches that regularly hire guest musicians to accompany their choir anthems, or venues that offer wedding packages, or even restaurants or department stores that hire.

Finally, there are local contractors that hire for touring musicals or backing orchestras for artists who come through town. Depending on the size of your community, there might be a lot of potential musical opportunities!

My own orchestra is a part time, regional group. But as a freelancer, as a substitute or extra musician, I have played with the Chicago Symphony, the Lyric Opera of Chicago, and the Milwaukee Symphony. I went on the Joffrey Ballet's tour to NYC. I've played with the Rochester Philharmonic, the Omaha Symphony, the Fort Wayne Philharmonic, the Indianapolis Chamber Orchestra. I've played behind *The Who,* Johnny Mathis, Art Garfunkel, *Mannheim Steamroller,* Andrea Bocelli, and so many other artists. I played on Oprah's show! Being a freelancer is a great way to enjoy artistic opportunities in organizations you haven't actually won auditions for, yet.

When you are taking auditions for full-time jobs, you can't control when or where you wind up winning. You might have to move across the country. When you do that, you might lose the students, the colleagues, the network you've built up in your previous life.

If you center your life in a freelance area, though, you can keep evolving through regional orchestras until your career has the right balance for you of commuting, artistry, income, and liveability. You can make choices!

HOW TO FREELANCE

If you are just getting started, here are some thoughts on breaking into the freelance scene.

Be in a place where there is a freelance scene. Yes, you can create your own opportunities wherever you are. But if your goal is to have some of your income streams be based around orchestral performing, or playing in opera pits or accompanying musical theater, you can't live in a tiny town with one community orchestra and two churches. You need a metropolitan area.

Make yourself visible. Have a website or a YouTube channel that a quick Google of your name will bring up. Make sure that the easiest thing to find is you, playing well and appearing to be a grownup. Visibility is difficult and scary for everyone, but it is crucial. I promise I'll talk more about this later.

Find out who the contractors are. They are personnel managers of orchestras, local giggers, churches that frequently hire musicians. Reach out politely and share your contact information and a little bit about yourself. A resume would be standard here, but make sure your communication is human and warm. These cold asks may not amount to anything at first, but at least they'll have your info. Sometimes they just need an oboist now! They'll go down their list—and *voila!*—you'll have an in.

Attend concerts, and after the concerts talk to the players. Find the ones that play your instrument and compliment them—genuinely—and make yourself known, then reach out to them and play for them. This will take time! But it will also be enjoyable and you may learn something.

You may want a bigger, better gig than the one in your local community. You may still be taking auditions. And you should keep working for that. But meanwhile? Work. Get some experience, play some rep, sit in some orchestras and understand how the interpersonal stuff works and how to be a professional: how to prepare, how to fake when needed, how to get the job done.

Make sure the local players of your instrument have your contact information. If they need someone at the last minute, your name and number should be on their list.

When you get that call or email, respond immediately and professionally. A professional response could be accepting the gig, asking a clarifying question, or politely declining. But your professionalism is apparent in how easy you are to work with. No contractor needs your life story, just a yes or a no. The most ambiguous response I would ever give is, "Thank you for the offer! I'd love to make this work but I have a conflict I'm trying to resolve on my end. May I let you know by Monday if I am available?" Don't let it be a pain to hire you. Fast, clear response is key.

When you get to the gig, be early. Arriving at the time of the rehearsal is late. Ten minutes before the downbeat is borderline late. You should be in your chair, warmed up, with a pencil on the stand and your restroom needs met well before the tuning note. You should have looked at your music, listened to a recording (or studied a score!), and you should be prepared to play every note. Sight reading in a professional orchestra rehearsal is not a good move. You will be exposed.

While you are there, be delightful and friendly. Pay attention, fit in, be a good colleague, and try to stay under the radar. Unless you have a solo turn—in which case, be awesome!

• • •

This is all obvious information. What's really interesting here is not getting the gig, but creating your career around the gig. It's hard to make your living from performing alone, even though that's traditionally been the musician's dream. Even before the pandemic shut down all live performances, this was hard. You can make between $300 and $1000 a week doing the freelancer dance of traveling from orchestra to orchestra, but it is grueling work unless you happen to magically live less than an hour away from multiple gig sources.

If your income comes from performing alone, it is inherently limited. You only have so many hours in a day, you only have so many Saturday nights in a week, and you can only play one gig at a time.

Consider your career as a set of numerous income streams and you'll find yourself in a much more secure position. Perhaps on the side, you teach. Or you compose, or you make arrangements for other musicians to play. Maybe you have some recording equipment and you set it up to capture other people's audition tapes. You might explore some of your other interests outside of music, even. Can you code? Can you build websites? Can you edit other people's manuscripts, can you cook, can you wait tables? Can you sell?

Having alternate income streams is smart for a million reasons, but the greatest one is that it takes the pressure off your playing. You don't have to take that one gig that's too far away, you don't have to play for that one conductor who makes your skin crawl, and you can choose to have an easy week between multiple busy ones.

This assumes you can accurately assess far enough ahead. I'm the queen of taking work that looks good on paper and then kicking myself when the level of difficulty plus the commute plus jury week for my students plus a recital I have to prepare all come together at once.

When you are trying to build your network, you want to take everything you are offered. But the more experience you get, the more you are allowed to have standards, and the more you are allowed to consider what you really want to be doing.

MORE THAN ONE WAY IN

My husband and I have a running joke, based in truth. Every job I've had I've gotten by playing. I auditioned for and won something. Or someone at a gig heard me play and invited me to play something else. I've kept these jobs because I am reliable and easy to get along with. But my personality and reliability on their own have never gotten me a gig.

Steve, on the other hand, has gotten every job he has by drinking beer with somebody. My husband meets people well and is a delight at parties, and has often been hired without ever being heard. He keeps those jobs by being a terrific player and a reliable gigger (though he's actually never won an audition). But he works steadily and is justifiably proud of his career.

The truism that I've heard is that to be a successful freelancer you must have two of three things: chops, reliability, a good personality. You can work if you're a great player and a great person but sometimes a little flaky. You can work if you're super nice and super reliable but only okay on your instrument. And you can work if you're a jerk but a fantastic player who never subs out or misses anything. Of course, I'd challenge you, as I challenge myself, to be all three! Why not put that effort in?

FREELANCER MATH

I was pleased and honored to be asked to go on tour. With a Polish song and dance group! It was four or five days, and it paid quite well—maybe $800 or $1000. This was early in my professional career, and seemed like it might be a big break.

Well. It was a tour to Erie PA, Cleveland, and Detroit. We were transported on a school bus, two to a seat. It was snowing the whole time. We were put up in shared hotel rooms. We were fed, family-style, at Polish restaurants in each community. I felt oversaturated with encased meats by the third day, but I had learned from the cautionary example of the one vegetarian in the group who had requested a veggie meal and was served—and this is true—a half a head of plain raw cabbage with a knife stuck in it.

There was not a minute of alone time, and the music was easy to the point of being uninteresting. When I got home, I had a cold and I was exhausted, on edge, bored, frustrated, and prepared to give up freelancing forever.

But I've been on tours since then that were wonderful, and I've been on tours since then that were at least acceptable, and I've been on tours that at least made for good stories.

When I am approached for work, I think seriously about what is being offered. I try to read between the lines as well. I learned from this "glamorous tour" that there are more important things to me than money. I learned to be thoughtful about the work versus the tradeoffs. I learned to pay attention to what I need to thrive. This gig wasn't that!

When you are asked to play a job, you need to know some things. Where, when, and what does it pay? These are absolute givens, right?

If you don't have that information, you can't respond with your availability. What repertoire? and Who is asking? are also relevant questions, but beginning freelancers might be advised to consider those secondarily.

There's one more "W" word: Why? This is obviously a bigger question, but has relevance in the overall context of your portfolio career.

Why are you taking freelance work at all? Why would you take this gig? Are you working to gain experience and to become a professional by being exposed to professionals? Are you already confident in your skills but taking gigs for extra money? Are you proud of the fact that your living is coming in exclusively from music? Are you trying to keep in shape between auditions? Are you trying to connect with musicians in your community? It's not necessary to agonize about these questions every time you get an offer, but it is worth being aware of your own answers and how they might be changing over time.

For years I was looking for work, ready and delighted to show up for any little job available to me. Over time, I became more and more choosy, because I could. But I still found myself sort of torn around every offer, because I hadn't thought through these ideas. So a part of my brain never wanted to say no.

I was afraid to say no, afraid that this gig was the last one I'd ever be offered. The scarcity mindset of the freelance musician is a hard one to overcome, and reasonably so. Work tends to come in surges. We build our bank accounts in the spring to live through the summer when jobs are slower. It's true that when your income changes from week to week and month to month, there's an argument for leaning into the busy when you can.

But it's liberating to have a rubric. If I know that what I am seeking now is artistic gratification, and what that means to me, I can cheerfully reject gigs that don't meet that threshold. I'd always prefer not to back out of a job I've agreed to, so I make a practice now of not accepting jobs that I would prefer not to play.

How much money is enough for me to accept the work? I think about how far away the job is, how many hours I'll have to spend in the car relative to the amount of playing I'll do, and whether the pay accounts for the gas and tolls. Some jobs sound good on paper, but barely cover the babysitter's wage when all is said and done, and that is allowed to be a factor.

Childcare is expensive and my husband and I came down on different sides of that equation. I don't mind taking a break-even gig if the repertoire is exciting to me, or if the people I'm going to be working with are kindred spirits, or if it's a new-to-me orchestra that I want to have contact with. My daughter won't be young forever, but I'll be a musician forever, and my network is my wealth. Steve is more engaged with the bottom line. He'd rather have the downtime at home than go out to work effectively for free if the job he's been offered conflicts with mine.

You are allowed to make the decision that is right for you.

DON'T PLAY FOR FREE

Should you accept free gigs? Jobs that pay in "exposure"? Generally, I think not. If you are just starting out in a new community, and you want to meet the musicians in town and have them hear you play, I can see the argument, but I'd counter that the people you meet doing free gigs are the people who are already doing free gigs. What work are they going to be able to offer you going forward? More free gigs?

Playing for free devalues the work that we do as musicians. If highly trained, highly skilled professional musicians are available for pittance wages or for nothing, why would anyone pay? And we need to be paid. Even work we love to do is work that has value.

As you begin your freelancing career, the math is around your time, your contacts, your musical development, and your own wishes. It is possible for freelance orchestral (and chamber, and pit) playing to be your entire income, but this is a difficult thing to sustain. If performance is the only thing that brings money in, what do you do if you are sick or injured? Or if you are tired? Or if the phone doesn't ring for a few weeks at a time? Or if a global pandemic eliminates all performances worldwide for a year?

Your portfolio career should involve more income streams than orchestral performance alone. Let's look at what that could be. Could you also be starting to give recitals? Creating a web presence? What are your next steps?

SPOTLIGHT ON A CAREER

RENÉE-PAULE GAUTHIER

Renée-Paule Gauthier is a passionate performer, teacher, and certified high-performance and life coach whose career has taken her across the United States and Canada as a soloist, recitalist, chamber musician, orchestral leader, and clinician.

In her work as a high-performance and life coach, Dr. Gauthier helps musicians gain clarity, unleash their full potential, and reach their desired outcome in their careers and lives.

She blogs about creating a meaningful practice at her website, Mind Over Finger, and hosts the Mind Over Finger podcast. The podcast offers discussions on mindful music-making, efficient practice, and building a purposeful career with the performers, pedagogues, and innovators who are shaping the classical music world today. Dr. Gauthier presents masterclasses and clinics on the topics of mindful practice, audition preparation, and anxiety management to audiences across the world.

RENÉE, HOW WOULD YOU DESCRIBE YOUR CURRENT WORK?

I have always worn many hats. The main description

started with violinist. Then I added teacher, arts administrator, podcaster, content creator, and now performance and life coach for musicians.

It has been wonderful to pursue all of these areas, and it has been incredible to find that my creativity is not linked only to the notes I produce out of my violin. I feel creative in all of these endeavors. In every concert I organize, in every sentence I write, in every exercise I invent for a student, in every question I craft for a client. I feel the ability to be creative and to express myself in all of these areas.

HOW DID YOU START DOING WHAT YOU DO?

I'm from a family of musicians, unsurprisingly. I followed the beaten path of the career violinist: music school, summer camps, competitions, college, auditions, and a performing career, playing solo, chamber music and orchestral repertoire. But one thing that impacted me tremendously is the fact that my mother ran a nonprofit music school. She is a formidable entrepreneur and leader in the nonprofit world. She has brought her magical touch to every project she's ever led. I grew up under her desk, watching her go. I believe that witnessing her brilliant creative mind, her attention to detail, and the way she handled stumbling blocks seeped into every pore of my body and shaped who I am. It is, I would say, only normal that I've always started projects wherever I went, from founding a chamber music festival, to starting a podcast, to creating online programs.

WHAT DO YOU LOVE ABOUT YOUR WORK?

The people, above all, and the personal interest of digging deeply into topics I'm curious and passionate about. Of course, hearing that audiences enjoy my playing is wonderful. But watching my students and my coaching clients blossom in front of my eyes is my favorite!

WHAT IS THE MOST CHALLENGING ASPECT OF YOUR CAREER?

For me, the most challenging aspects of my life is and has always been the same: the unstable schedule and income. As a human being, I thrive on continuity and routine. The life of a portfolio musician is nothing continuous and routine-like!

WHAT BARRIERS DID YOU HAVE TO OVERCOME TO GET TO WHERE YOU ARE?

Had you asked this question a couple of years ago, I could have found a lot of external barriers. But the more I journey through life, the more I realize that the barriers are all self-imposed by my limiting self-beliefs, my fears, my insecurities, and every single time I chose to accept the rules imposed on me by others. Thanks to years of coaching and thought work, I now see that I have so much agency in my life.

WHAT ADVICE WOULD YOU GIVE TO SOMEONE THAT WANTED TO HAVE A CAREER LIKE YOURS?

Take ownership of your career. Take ownership of your learning experience. I see young students making the mistake of thinking that whichever degree they are enrolled in will fully prepare them for the life ahead. That is delusional. Do the work—the internal work. Ask yourself and answer the hard question: What do you truly want? And, once you know, find the tools to get it.

Appreciate what you are getting from your environment, your school, your teachers. Then find the gaps, the areas where you want more skills, and develop them. Work with coaches, read books, watch tutorials. Be interested. Be invested in your own life.

Don't wait for others to provide you with the answers. And, mostly, follow the breadcrumbs. Have big, bold dreams and pursue them tenaciously, but follow your instinct and interests as well. They could take you somewhere extraordinary.

IS THERE ANYTHING YOU WOULD LIKE TO ADD?

Everyone should get a coach!

6

Creating a Solo Career

It is hard to play the oboe. It's hard to play any instrument at a really high level, of course. But the oboe is difficult to start, and the learning curve is... rough. Early on you do so much struggling against the reed, against the resistance of the instrument, against the antiquated fingering system. As you begin to learn to make your own reeds, you slowly gain more control of the instrument and the sound you are making but then, suddenly, half or more of your practice time is devoted to carpentry rather than artistry, and all around you violinists and pianists and trumpet players get to spend their time practicing while you are just at a desk building your instrument.

All this is to say that when I entered a concerto competition in my senior year of high school, it was not the case that I'd done a ton of competition playing. I was a band and orchestra performer. I went to Solo and Ensemble every year, once a year. But I would not say that I was an experienced soloist.

I was *terribly* nervous. I kept trying my reed and then putting it away again, itching to play more because doing something is satisfying, knowing that I shouldn't risk exhausting my embouchure before I played. I did not have a relaxing playlist or a mantra or any of the mindset hacks that we adults know about now. I had no idea whether the performance would go well or not, and it could easily not have. The oboe is dangerous. Live performance is dangerous. I was definitely going to walk off the stage alive, but you couldn't know that from my stress response.

And then it was my turn.

From the opening three piano notes, I was *in*. Like a canoe sliding into the water, I was in the music and playing it just like I heard it in my head. I didn't feel like I was the one doing the playing, even; I was just hearing it and out it came. I was fully in the moment—not locked into a rigid, rehearsed interpretation of the piece, but able to flow, to micro-improvise, to stretch here and push there.

You can't ever ignore the traps of the oboe, but my kinetic awareness was one step ahead the whole time, predicting where it would fight me and heading it off. It felt like I couldn't miss, like the entire concerto was running through me, like all I had to do was stand back and allow it.

There is no recording of this competition. I did win it, but I doubt my performance was flawless, or that it was anything other than an 18-year-old's rendition of the Vaughan Williams Oboe Concerto. I've heard 18-year-olds play this piece since then. I'll say no more.

But the actual playing of it, that experience where I was not controlling but in control, where I was not working hard but everything was working, where I was fully in the music and also making the music. This is *Flow.*

FLOW

This is the first time I remember being in this flow state. It's addictive. Like a drug, but it never loses its magic. All of the practicing I do now, all of the work I put in behind the scenes, is designed to create the conditions, the opportunity for flow. I don't take it for granted. I welcome it when it comes.

I became a professional musician because I loved to play the oboe. That hasn't changed. But over time I've discovered that, in the same way that bread is useful to me primarily as a vehicle for delivering butter, the thing I love about the oboe is actually the way it facilitates my path into the flow state.

Flow is that state of optimal concentration and absorption described by Mihaly Csikszentmihalyi in numerous works. It's that feeling you get when you are lost in the music and in your own world. That feeling of timelessness, of effortlessness, of channeling something better than me is what I seek, what I strive for. It's what I chase when I'm practicing and performing. There's no better high for me.

Musicians never get to a point where they dust off their hands and think, "Yup, I'm perfect now. No more improvement can possibly be made. I have practiced all I need to." There is always deeper understanding to pursue, greater mastery.

At 83, the great cellist Pablo Casals was asked why he continued to practice four and five hours a day. Casals answered, "Because I think I am making progress."

I can find flow in my practice room when I'm working on something with just the right amount of challenge. I can lose myself in the fascinating creative, technical, and intellectual search for solutions. This is the same kind of flow that I can feel when I'm solving a crossword puzzle, or just before a Sudoku breaks itself open. It's when the solution is not yet known, but when I know I can achieve it. It's the joy of the difficulty of the process.

I can also find it while performing, writing, or teaching. It's when all of the effortful intellectual challenge seems to drop away, and I feel *Flow* as a channeling through me. The music seems to be coming through me, through my instrument, without me having to *work* to make it. When I teach from my flow state I find myself saying things that are true but that I didn't know I knew.

Sometimes other people can provide me with flow. It's like a contact high when my colleagues are playing so well that all I have to do is ride on their energy. I discount this version, sometimes, because I don't generate it myself. But the magic is the same.

Even in this third case, I can't reliably get to a flow state just by luck. I have to show up prepared, relaxed, focused, and stay in the moment. And even then sometimes it doesn't come. But I crave it every time.

Flow, or the possibility of it, is what keeps me coming back to the oboe, to my desk, to my creative habits day after day, year after year. It's an important ingredient in my life that makes me feel alive. I don't get tired of searching for it—I don't get tired of my jobs—because the possibility always exists of finding a flow moment.

• • •

After that high school concerto competition, I knew for sure that I was going forward into a career in music, and that being a soloist was the path for me.

You'll notice, though, that when I talk about my playing career it's largely about orchestral playing. It's easier to start out by doing gigs with established ensembles than it is to become a household name all on your own. It's more straightforward to take an orchestral audition than it is to find a way through all the noise of the internet to be known as yourself.

You don't—usually—get booked by major artist management right out of school. You have to do a lot of self-promotion and career development on your own to get there. Agents don't pick up people who don't have an audience, and I had assumed that I couldn't develop an audience until I had an agent.

Again, should my music conservatory have taught me something— anything—about how to build an audience, how to promote my own concerts, how to market myself in the way I wanted? Of course. Did it? Not at all.

After school, I applied to a few agencies. I entered some competitions. I got nowhere, because of course, I was at that time, nobody.

Looking back now, I see that my shyness and introversion and a certain fixed-mindset pride kept me from reaching out. I didn't dare to tell anybody what I really wanted, lest I be disappointed by their rejection. I silently moved through my life, trying to do my jobs as best I could, hoping to be noticed, discovered, invited. I let my playing speak for me, but I never spoke for myself. I had to change before I could have the opportunities I wanted.

But you know what I did know how to do? I knew how to play the oboe. So I got myself a pianist and we booked a church and I gave a performance. My friends, his friends, and a couple of church-goers came. And then later a college I was adjuncting at offered me an (unpaid) recital hall slot and I did another performance. And as I did these tiny performances every few months, I learned new repertoire, I began to identify my own performing style, and I began to build up a small following.

I began by giving the kinds of academic recitals I was taught to do in school, where you walk onstage, bow, play a lengthy work of serious music, bow, and leave. But I soon found that the audience had more fun—and that I did too!—when I talked to them. I introduced the pieces, shared why I loved them, gave them things to listen for, helped them to relate to the lesser-known works I was performing. I began to theme my recitals and to keep the audience's experience in mind as I programmed them. Maybe I didn't need to play every movement of every work? Maybe the arc of the program was best if I put the hardest piece last, or in the middle, or whatever? I only play pieces I like, but I play them for the audience, and I always keep the audience in mind.

Eventually, I figured out how to collect email addresses and start a professional email list. When I performed, I let my audience know, and some of them came! Eventually, I began reaching out to organizations that had existing recital series so my performances got in front of increasingly large audiences. I started a Facebook page which was a step toward claiming myself as a professional soloist. Not a full-time soloist, but someone who had things to announce and share.

This Facebook page was a big trigger for my imposter syndrome. None of my orchestral colleagues had created professional pages. I didn't see anyone around me trying to promote themselves in this way. Every time I made a post on that page I had to steel myself, click "post", and then slam the computer shut and walk away to recover. It was scary for me, but I did it because I wanted to be seen.

Since then, I have grown to love social media. I can talk with people all over the world, I can reach an audience larger than my small town, and when things get to be too much for my introverted self, I can take a little break. There are plenty of other things for people to engage with; they won't miss me for a week if I get busy. It's got all the best qualities of being social with none of the actual social awkwardness of in-person me.

But the brave step of *saying* I was a soloist was the step I needed. People believe what you tell them, and they believe you if you act like a soloist.

My own orchestras offered me concertos to play. It's in everyone's interest, right? They can pay me less than a managed artist whom they have to fly in and house. They can bring focus to a member of their own orchestra to make their audience feel like they know me. And I can get what I want, which is the flow experience of performing with an orchestra.

I love this. I'm easy to work with because I come prepared, I give a good show, and I don't have a big ego. I'm very unfussy, so they ask me back again and again.

As I became less shy about publicizing these events, I became visible as an oboist who would show up and play concertos, and so other orchestras asked me to play with them.

Nowadays, when I plan a recital event, I look for at least four different venues to perform in, ideally more like six. I might do one of those for free, at a college where I teach, for example, but I expect the others to pay substantially enough to make my collaborators and me happy. I advertise these to my email list, on my social media, and in the local papers, and I expect my venues to help in that publicity. I have been a featured soloist for a number of smaller orchestras. I get paid to show up on stage, talk about my pieces, and present interesting repertoire that I love.

Are big-time soloists playing little jobs like this? Maybe not; maybe this is small-potatoes stuff. But is it bringing me joy? Is it keeping me challenged? Is it sharing 20th and 21st century oboe music with new audiences? Is it making me money? *Yes!*

No one has to do the same things I have done; there are faster tracks to moderate success than the paths I've trod. But here's my important point.

Your way doesn't have to be perfect right away. When you start out, it's all right for it to be kind of improvisational, for there to be mistakes and real misses. You might show up and give a stellar performance for two people. You might be in front of 50 and mess up. It's all part of the learning curve, and it's OK to evolve toward the thing you want.

If you had told me when I was 20 years old that I'd give ten to twelve solo recital and concerto performances every year, for real audiences, and get paid for them? I'd have said that was my dream and asked what the catch was.

No catch. I just started out where I was—with my shyness and my nervousness and my total lack of understanding about how to publicize a concert, how to do ticket sales, how to develop a career—and I learned as I went along. There is no shame in being who you are, where you are. But if you have a vision of where you want to go, you can just keep leaning toward that.

CASE STUDY IN HUSTLE

Here's a story I'm proud of. I was invited to perform the Ewazen concerto, *Down a River of Time,* with a small regional orchestra in downstate Illinois. The invitation came about because the operations manager of the orchestra was also a violinist in another small regional orchestra downstate—the orchestra in which I'd gotten my professional start. She knew me and had heard my concerto performances before, so when they were looking for a wind soloist to give variety to their season, she suggested me. My website still looked pretty homemade, but it was enough to give me some legitimacy, and they reached out and booked me.

The money they offered was fine, but I wondered if there might be more I could do with this trip. I suggested that they could use me outside the orchestra services to do some musical outreach, and they came through beautifully, setting up a small meet-and-greet-and-play at a local senior center, a radio interview, and a masterclass for local oboe students. *Wonderful!* But there was still some time in my schedule, so I reached out to two other people that I knew—a youth orchestra director in Springfield and the oboe professor in Normal. On the two days off between events, I drove a couple of hours and gave two more masterclasses. Both groups paid me.

Does that all sound like a lot of work? It was, but what a pleasure! I got to meet lots of oboists. I got to give performances and speak to the public. Several of the oboists I met are still in my circle, ordering reeds or reaching out with questions. I got to reconnect with people I had lost touch with. And I had an absolute blast. It felt like a real performing tour, and I was proud to have set it all up for myself, just by hustling and connecting and reaching out.

Look, I'm writing this book in the 11th month of the United States' COVID lockdown. We are not out having orchestra concerts yet, and nothing is the same. But during this time I've managed to perform—and get paid—eight times. Some of those performances have been livestreams from home with a virtual tip jar. Some have been outdoors for distanced audiences. Some have been streamed by real chamber series, established to support musicians. Nothing is impossible.

NOW YOU TRY

As always, your dream career doesn't need to look like mine. But it's good to think about these questions.

GET CLEAR

- Do you want to create performances outside of orchestral work? Do you crave more artistic freedom?
- What kind of performance would you give if you were fully in control? If you had an audience there, what would you offer them? Would it be chamber music? Solo work? Would it be an orchestra concert that was just... different in some way? Would it be a poetry reading?
- What would you do if you knew you couldn't fail?

JUST START

Now that you have an idea of what this amazing project might look like, you can brainstorm the first steps toward creating it.

- Who is the audience? Can you think of two or three people you already know who would love this? Where are they? Are they in your town, in the next big city over, or are they online?
- What collaborators might you need? Do you have some of them already identified in your mind?
- Where might you do this? Do you have a venue in mind? This might be a good time to do some googling, or some ASKING. (I toured one of my recitals all the way to Philadelphia by reaching out to a presenter recommended by an old friend!)

LET IT EVOLVE

Is this something you could do right now, or something you will need to build up to? What might a first step toward it look like? A mini performance that begins to build an audience? A trial run?

What is stopping you? What makes you hesitate about this dream of yours?

Here is a brief list of things you might be thinking:

- I am too young.
- I am too old.
- I am too scared.
- I am not good enough.
- I don't have enough experience.
- I don't have a website.
- I would need new headshots to do this.
- I need to be someone different.

I hear you. I see you. I know this is how it feels. I have felt these things, too. And none of it matters. You don't need to be a finished product yet; it's OK to be who you are, where you are. If you have something to share, share it! It will get easier over time; you can build a website and a press kit later. If the dream you have is meant to happen, you can't mess it up. If you start and you hate it, you'll know.

You don't have to spend a fortune as you are learning how to deliver great concerts. It can be expensive to book a venue, pay a collaborator, and advertise an event. It can be cheap or free to produce something at home and share it on YouTube and work your networks to drive traffic to it. I'm a believer in getting your artistry out there in the world—and also a believer in not going into debt while you are just starting out.

Similarly, I'm a huge proponent of new music and I recently commissioned a piece for the first time. That, it turns out, is very expensive. Offering a second or a third performance of a new work is still a service to the world, and a composer might be delighted to have that happen, and you could still be at the front of the line and get very visible by being one of the only existing recordings.

ASK FOR HELP

Do you need some help? Reach out. No matter how unique your idea is, something like it has been created before, and someone has some experience in making it happen. You could ask your teacher, or a mentor from your community. You could reach out to me through my website, jennetingle.com. Nothing is unsolvable.

PLEASE NOTE

There's a huge difference between "Don't build a whole website for this yet," and "Don't bother to promote your event." If you want an audience you definitely have to invite people to come. You have to make it sound fun and exciting. You have to find your people where they are. Can you post flyers at your school? Is your audience following you on social media already? Is there a group on your preferred social platform that would be super interested in this? A hashtag that might attract the right people? It can be really difficult to get attention for your project, but that challenge is the work!

It is OK to be creative. Think about what you want to put out into the world. Think about who would want to see or hear it. And then brainstorm ways to get it done. There are potential collaborators in your circle and people out in the world who would love what you have to offer. Performance is such a generous act, and more complexity does not necessarily translate to higher quality. What if you just shared your music with someone, somehow, and then built from there?

Remember, though, that performance is only one way to succeed. Yes, I've devoted three chapters to it just now. I love to perform. But the Portfolio Career, at its best, has other elements that fall more under your own control. Let's look at what those could be.

7

Creating a Business

An oboe reed is a delicate little thing. It's made of bamboo, cork, brass, and thread, and hand-crafted to the specification of the performer.

The reed is the only part of the oboe that actually produces sound. The most expensive, high-quality instrument can still sound like a goose if the reed is not up to the task.

The reed is made of organic material, and has a short lifespan, during which it is constantly changing: reacting to humidity and barometric pressure, stiffening as it dries and breaking down over prolonged periods of soaking and drying, and exposure to the enzymes in our mouths. The reed affects the sound, pitch, articulation, and resistance of the oboe.

Making reeds is a time-consuming process, involving machines, tools, and extensive skilled hand-scraping. Ideally, it takes place over three to four days to allow sufficient soaking and drying time. We are oboists because we love the sound, the tonal possibilities, the artistry of making music. But we are forced to spend half our time at our desks, messing around with little pieces of damp wood.

It's highly skilled work, and I was well-trained and fairly competent at it when I graduated from school. I got a lot better and more efficient after that, as you'll read, but the process didn't stress me out too much.

Reed-making stresses some people out enormously, though, and young students can't make their own reeds (you don't give sharp knives to 6th graders!), so teachers can get overwhelmed with the needs of their studio. Many people simply don't have the time to devote to learning how to make good reeds.

Therefore, the business I'll talk about in this chapter was a natural fit for me. Something I was already doing was helpful to others, and I created an income from it.

A reed-making business is specific to oboists—maybe bassoonists, maybe clarinetists?—but as you read, I'd invite you to think about something you could do or make that would be a benefit to people like you.

I know a woman who makes and sells fabric mute bags that hang over your chair—so the mutes are always an easy reach away. I see people creating hooks to take the weight of the instrument, or making better thumb rests, or re-hairing bows. In our current times, there's a market for orchestral PPE: masks through which you can play an instrument, bell covers, etc.

My oboe reed business didn't start out like much. My origin story is very much of its time, and resonant with the way I tackle things in my life: small, then evolving messily and with no real intention toward success. I got smarter and savvier, but in the beginning I just took the steps that presented themselves.

I started out making reeds for one person. She was an active freelancer, much higher on the "ladder" than I was at the time. She was rehabbing from a hand injury and couldn't keep up with her own reed-making needs, so she hired me to make them for her.

I charged her something like $10 or $12 per reed. I made her five or ten every week, and I drove to her house to deliver them in person. As part of my service, I filed down and greased the corks to make them easier to insert and remove.

This was a lot of work for not that much money. But I was also in my 20s, living in the world's tiniest apartment, trying to break into the scene, and her checks netted me much more per hour than my minimum wage day job did.

I was making reeds for myself anyway, right? It wasn't much more effort to make a few extra in every session, and every little bit of income helped.

As her hand problems resolved—after several years working together—she went back to making her own reeds, and I missed the sense of purpose, the income, and most of all the efficiency.

There's a big difference between making reeds just for yourself and making them for yourself and others. If I'm working only for myself, I prepare only as many as I think I'll need, and then try to make each one a gem.

In contrast, if I'm trying to make a case full of basic, competent reeds, I can go a lot faster. I can enjoy some economies of scale. I can batch process and let my reeds be on an assembly line of sorts.

Because of this efficiency, I wind up with a high percentage of good reeds with a lot less emotional attachment. For me, a reed business was a fantastic way to hone my skills and improve my processes, independent of the actual income.

Have you read that story about the ceramics teacher? I feel like I see it everywhere. It's from the book *Art and Fear,* by David Bayles and Ted Orland.

> The ceramics teacher announced on opening day that he was dividing the class into two groups. All those on the left side of the studio, he said, would be graded solely on the quantity of work they produced, all those on the right solely on its quality. His procedure was simple: on the final day of class he would bring in his bathroom scales and weigh the work of the "quantity" group: 50 pounds of pots rated an "A", 40 pounds a "B", and so on. Those being graded on "quality", however, needed to produce only one pot —albeit a perfect one—to get an "A".
>
> Well, came grading time and a curious fact emerged: the works of highest quality were all produced by the group being graded for quantity. It seems that while the "quantity" group was busily churning out piles of work—and learning from their mistakes—the "quality" group had sat theorizing about perfection, and in the end had little more to show for their efforts than grandiose theories and a pile of dead clay.

In other words, making more reeds was good for me financially *and* artistically. So I wanted more customers.

I wrote a letter, printed out 100 copies on paper with an order form on the back, stuffed them into envelopes, and mailed them, with stamps and handwritten addresses, to every oboist in the Chicago Federation of Musicians Union Directory. This was a weird time, right? The late 90s? It's not that the internet didn't exist, but social media certainly didn't, and the thought of having my own website wasn't even a concept in my mind. I barely had an email address. I came out of college without having had any online experiences (conservatory education, mid-90s). Reaching out globally was not a thing I considered.

But listen: it is indeed a good business idea to reach out to people who know you to find your first clients, to people who are in the very specific niche that you want to serve. On the one hand, I can laugh at my 24-year-old self licking a hundred envelopes. On the other hand, if I were going to start something new right now, I'd look for the people in my life who might be interested and contact them directly. It was a savvy move, clunkily executed.

But I got a customer. Then a few weeks later, I got another. Then the first customer sent some students to me for reeds. And it wasn't too long before my business started growing, all by word of mouth.

I made some smart business moves early on, without knowing anything or strategizing in advance.

I rapidly enabled a monthly reed subscription service. Normally, you would send me a check in the mail for reeds, after which I would make the reeds and send them out to you, and the whole process would take a few weeks. But if you subscribed, you would get a small discount, and I would send your reeds reliably on the 5th of the month and invoice you. The advantage to you? Consistent filling of your reed case. The advantage to me? Predictable work flow and predictable income. I've tweaked this process many times over the last 20 years, but I still offer a (technologically improved) version of that subscription service. It's a win-win. The lesson: look for ways to make it easier for your people, and for you!

I discovered that if I sent out a friendly letter to people who had ordered before, with an order form on the back (still in an envelope with a stamp, because tech was slow to develop for me), I would get an influx of orders. In this way, a tiny newsletter was born. The lesson: communicating with your people is important, and magical, and basically always a good thing for them and for you. It's worth the effort to stay at the top of your customer's mind.

I discovered that when I bumped my prices up by a dollar or so every few years, I had a lot of personal feelings about it. A lot of anxiety, a lot of fear. But those feelings never translated to reduced sales. Feelings around money are normal—and I still struggle with them—but it literally never happened that someone saw my reed prices go up by a dollar and called to yell at me. In fact, as my prices went up, my business grew. The lesson: money is a mental game. The agonies you go through around your pricing don't have to translate to agony for others.

I discovered that it was useful to track my reeds and orders and customers, and I created a spreadsheet that gave me all of the information I needed. It was imperfect, and unsearchable, but I'm using a version of that same spreadsheet today. I briefly tried to move to a much more professional customer and inventory management system, but it proved to be more than I needed for my purposes, and it was so complex I couldn't manage it myself. My tracking system is clunky, but with it I can follow the trends I need to follow. The lesson: keep it simple and let your systems be what you need them to be.

I eventually learned to create a basic website, slowly figured out how to accept payments online, and then gradually improved and added to and built up my own site until I outgrew my own tech skills and hired someone to redesign it. The lesson: it doesn't have to be great at first. Just make it easy for someone to find you and pay you!

If I could make my own first website, as a person who came of age before the internet, you certainly can, too.

As I got more comfortable with my systems and processes, as I began to know how to make my reed business fit into my life without stress, I wanted to grow it. I realized that selling a fully finished reed was actually limiting, as it meant my customers were only those who couldn't (or preferred not to) make reeds at all.

I wanted to reach oboists who were already making their own reeds, too. So I began to offer earlier stages of the process. Half-scraped reeds. Reed blanks. Processed cane. Unprocessed cane. Knives and tools and supplies. All of the things I had to have and create to get a finished reed out the door could be sold independently. They'd save someone plenty of time and effort, and as my business grew, I could really take advantage of those economies of scale. I could acquire cane more cheaply by buying it by the kilo from the grower. I could access dealer pricing on tools and supplies. The lesson: be creative and don't assume that people only want one version of the thing you do.

I experimented with online ads, and with advertising in our trade publication, but these didn't spark joy for me—or work terribly well. The oboe niche is very small, and word of mouth has always been my best driver. When I started my YouTube channel, though, my business really took off.

FIVE MINUTE REEDMAKER

I created the *Five Minute Reedmaker* video series in 2017, at first just to answer some of the questions I was getting. People would email me and say, "I loved the reeds you sent me, but they are too hard (too easy, too unstable, too closed, too open, etc.) for me. What should I do?"

This is not too surprising—reeds are very individual. What feels good to me might not work for another person I've never met. I wrote a lot of emails back, saying things like:

> "Thanks for getting in touch! I'm glad to have the opportunity to improve your experience. Can you be a little bit analytical about how the reed is too hard? If it's too hard in the response—slow to tongue on, but easy enough once it gets going—you would want to scrape in the tip, from the "gutters" of the rooftop up to the corners. If it's too hard in the sustain—you can start a note easily but have to work hard to maintain sound quality—you might want to very gently polish the heart area. If it's too open you might want to squish it with your fingers (after it's thoroughly soaked, of course) and try again. Too flat in the high register (and thus exhausting to play) you might wish to clip a tiny bit. If you are not successful with these fixes, you can send it back to me and I'll try a second time to get you something that you can use. Let me know how it goes!"

I was pretty good at putting on this cheerful, helpful voice, instead of getting triggered by people not liking my reeds. But I definitely got tired of writing that email.

So I made some videos. What to do when your reed is too hard, too easy, unstable, etc.? Those got very popular, so I made more. So many more. I talked about the various stages of reed-making, the skills, and the adjustments I make. I gave away all of the information I could think of for free, on YouTube, and the more I gave away, the more people reached out to me with questions and also ordered from me. The lesson: be helpful! People want to learn, and if you can teach them, they see you as the expert.

It turns out that when you have helpful advice for people, and you show up and say so, people listen. I have built a great, joyful, and loving audience of oboists through that YouTube channel, and I've been listening to them and serving them ever since! They ask questions, I make videos to answer them, I get better at the work through having to break it down and describe what I'm doing, and they get the help they need. It's synergistic and energizing. The lesson: helping people helps you!

Before I started my channel, I ran a weekend Oboe Reed Boot Camp in summer, mostly for my own students, and had a few additional local folks enroll. We had a good time for several years. It was growing slowly by word of mouth.

The year after I started my channel, though, when I ran Boot Camp again, I was able to bring people together from much farther away. At its pre-pandemic peak, I was filling the room and meeting people from Texas, Colorado, and even Canada who came to South Bend to spend the weekend together and make reeds.

When I demonstrated skills, people caught me in mistakes and quoted me back to me. This is the power of building a following! What's the lesson here? When you have an audience, many things become possible.

Between my YouTube channel, my blog, and my weekly email newsletter, I have recently begun to feel like my main job in my business is creating content, and only secondarily creating reeds—and this feels fantastic to me. It keeps my life interesting, creative, and open, and everything I share is something that comes back to me.

I started by working with little bits of damp wood and created an entire community!

In 2019 my reed business income stream hit six figures. That top line dropped somewhat during the pandemic, but it's still a huge piece of my portfolio career.

This chapter is the story of my 21-year path to overnight success. To be clear, it did not have to take that long. I didn't have any vision for the business when I started it. I was looking to bring in a little extra income to help with the rent and groceries, not to build an empire. And for a long time, for years, that's exactly what I did. My business grew only through word of mouth, and developed very slowly. The workload was manageable around my playing and teaching, and it did enable me to leave my day job well before my performing career alone could have supported me. It gave my husband and me a feeling of stability as every week another two or three checks or deposits would show up. They were small, but they just kept coming, enhancing and confirming my feeling that the money would always come from somewhere.

I didn't have to start the YouTube channel that wound up dramatically growing my audience and customer base. I did that because it seemed like fun, because it was a pleasure for me to be creative in that way. I find, generally, that when I lean into the things that feel enjoyable to me, people respond well.

The lesson: I took something I was doing anyway—making reeds—and improved my skills by making a lot of them. I was adequate at reed-making when I started my business. I was getting by, but having to ship quality reeds regularly forced me to get consistent and fast. The more reeds I made, the better they got. Over time, I also evolved my sense of myself as a business owner. I got smarter and savvier about how to keep up with demand, how to market myself and my products, and how to communicate with my audience. And I turned the business into something very profitable. I have no background or training in business. If I could create this, you can, too!

NOW YOU TRY

Does any of this sound appealing to you? Could you imagine starting a small side business that supports your creative career, or is itself a part of your creative career? This is possible for you!

JUST START

What do you already do or create that feels easy and fun to you, but not to other people?

- Do you craft?
- Do you re-hair bows, or make mutes, or design breathable concert clothes?
- Can you write or edit artist bios?
- Can you build websites or apps?
- What things come so naturally and easily to you that you are surprised when you see someone else struggling?

Who are the people who might want that thing? Do you know anyone specific? Or can you paint a general picture of that person?

Has anyone else already made a business of that? It's not a bad thing if they have. There's room for everyone in a creative field!

Do some Googling, see what is being offered and what might be missing from that. Maybe what is missing is the *you* version of it!

What kind of pricing exists for this idea in the world? You don't have to base your pricing directly on other people's, but you do need to have a sense of what is appropriate.

- Want to charge more than the market? Find a way to position yourself as high end. Add more value to the offer. Make it better than anyone else's!
- Want to charge less? Why do you want that? If that reason isn't based simply on fear or scarcity, feel free. Just to find a way to make it more efficiently.

It's OK to start small and not have the entire industry built up around your offer. It's less OK to start and be unable to fulfill the orders you do get. But it would be awful to not start, if this sounds like fun. Find a workable first step and see what you can do.

Determine an offer and a price. You can change that price later as you learn more. Be careful about starting too low: it devalues the work, it might undercut other professionals, and it might make it more difficult to raise your prices later.

No one will reach out to you to ask about the thing you are dreaming up in your head. You have to tell them it exists. Reach out to someone who looks like an ideal client or customer. Talk with them about your offer. Ask if they know someone who might be interested. It might be them!

As you approach people, try to be helpful, interested, interesting, but neutral about the actual outcome. Desperation isn't attractive, and if the product or service you are offering is of high quality, it will find its market.

Really, action begets action. If you sell one item, it will be exciting. It will probably make you want to sell another. You'll think of a way to reach out and find another customer. You'll begin to think about how to reach people you don't know. You'll consider SEO and ads. Before you know it, you'll have a business! But you don't need to know the whole thing before you start.

Let me be clear that not every hobby has to be monetized! It's OK to have something you love to do just for you, that you don't need to offer to the world. It's OK to try to sell something and later decide that you don't want to.

What I do want for you, though, is the understanding that you have strengths and skills and brilliance, and that those are assets that have value. Creating a new income stream can create a measure of financial stability in your life, independent of performing, and you might love that.

Of course, most musicians start their portfolio careers by teaching. Let's talk about that next.

SPOTLIGHT ON A CAREER

AMANDA McINTOSH

For most of her life, Amanda McIntosh has been a clarinetist and something else. Those "something elses" have included: public relations assistant, translator, music critic, business process consultant, project manager, entrepreneur, social media consultant, and business trainer. She's also taught a lot of private clarinet lessons.

All of those "something elses" help her with her current company, *Take My Face Off*, which manufactures environmentally responsible alternatives to face wipes and cotton balls. She also works with Honesty Pill Coaching to help musicians market their businesses.

AMANDA, HOW WOULD YOU DESCRIBE YOUR CURRENT WORK?

I only perform these days when someone really great asks, or when it's repertoire I'm dying to play. I don't teach right now, but I do get to think about teaching-related challenges when I help my coaching clients. I love that.

I'm a businessperson who has to be a jill-of-all-trades. I spend most of my time on marketing. I have to keep all the plates spinning for our manufacturing workshop, our PR contractors, the Amazon store, and our own direct-to-consumer website. I spend most of my day writing marketing emails, reformatting images, creating social media content, and hammering out partnerships. For the coaching clients, I help them plan their messaging. Together, we write web copy, emails, and plan social media.

I actually love managing people, but our team is so small, I don't do a lot of that. I look forward to delegating more tasks in the future so I can focus more on the big picture.

HOW DID YOU START DOING WHAT YOU DO?

Re: *Take My Face Off,* I was driving home late from a concert and realized I was out of clean washcloths to take off my makeup. The skincare routine I relied on at the time required a clean washcloth every night, and I kept running out before laundry day. Every time I looked for new ones, I just found more of the same, gross ones I already owned and hated.

I have lots of ideas, but many of them seem complicated or unrealistic. This time, I thought, "How hard can it be to create a better washcloth? It's not rocket science!" Of course, it turned out to be super complicated. But once I realized my product had an environmental benefit, it became a mission.

I spent about a year researching and learning. Then I created a massive deadline for myself. I decided to show off Mittys at the world's biggest beauty trade show in Las Vegas. I created a whole brand and look, rented a tiny booth space, sewed my own prototypes, and went to Vegas. This led to Sephora licensing one of my designs.

For the coaching, it's just my personality to try and solve puzzles. And it's great that now I get paid to do it. (It's why I used to love audition preparation; it was a huge puzzle to solve and it had a big payoff.)

My problem-solving hobby got me into trouble in music school. The school director was sick and tired of my newspaper exposés on this or that topic. He wanted to refocus my energy by sending me off to New York for an internship in music criticism. I said "No!" Traditional music criticism seemed pointless. The way it was being done at the time, there were no problems being solved, no new audiences being reached. Critics were almost literally preaching to the choir.

I always felt out of place in music, but I loved playing. I went to grad school, took an orchestra job in Spain, then met my husband at Tanglewood, and eventually came back to the States. I then freelanced, auditioned, and worked as a business consultant all at the same time for years.

WHAT DO YOU LOVE ABOUT YOUR WORK?

I love marketing. People think marketing is "icky," but marketing is just effective communication towards a specific goal. If the goal is good, marketing feels great.

I love the challenge of spreading information that has a social benefit. My website, my marketing emails, my social media, the photo shoots, the interviews I give—they're all tools in this big campaign I'm on to get people to quit using disposable products. If they buy my product as a result, all the better. But even if they don't, it feels good to spread this information.

People bring different attention spans and expectations to each experience in their lives. If you take the time to get into their heads, really consider their experiences, you can figure out how to position your information so that they take notice and get some benefit from it.

Most of my work with coaching clients is getting them to look at their businesses the way their audience does. If they understand their audience's expectations, they'll create better work in fewer drafts. More impact, less effort.

WHAT IS THE MOST CHALLENGING ASPECT OF IT FOR YOU?

Getting past perfectionism. *Take My Face Off* is part of the beauty retail world. Thanks to classical music, I was already a perfectionist. Going into beauty and feeling completely out of place, I went into perfectionism overdrive. I spent a lot of time trying to do everything, and I thought it all had to be perfect. I wasted so much effort.

It took me years to figure out how to manage my effort better. I still struggle. You have to get really good at ignoring trends or people or advice that will distract you. You have to be comfortable doing things differently. You also have to be comfortable at being terrible at some things. Most of the time, done is better than good!

WHAT BARRIERS DID YOU HAVE TO OVERCOME TO GET TO WHERE YOU ARE?

External—time, money, knowledge. All of the normal stuff. I'm privileged enough that I was only working part-time (some music work, some consulting work) when I started my business. My kids were young, but I'm a terrible housekeeper, so there were some free hours in each day. I'm sure a tidier person wouldn't have been able to find the time.

Even though my husband was supporting the household, the "normal" way of starting my kind of business required much more money than we had. So I taught myself a lot of jobs to fill in the gaps. I learned about patent law. And manufacturing. And websites. And so on and so on, because I couldn't afford all the expert help I needed.

It was uncomfortable and challenging to find the funds to start my company. I recognize that there are people who have done much more with much less than I had, and find them truly awe-inspiring.

Internal—the doubters. Some people loved my work, but plenty of others have told me it was pointless, or that I was deluded, or that there wasn't any need for it in the world. Most of these people didn't know what they were talking about; some were experts.

At this one press interview (with a huge website), the 20-something journalist mocked me for suggesting the world needed more environmental products. It felt like high school all over again. One retail partner needed to break the news that they were going to carry a competitor's products instead of mine. I guess she was nervous, because instead of explaining, she gave me a list of reasons why I was awful and then ended the call. (I got the rest of the story later from someone else.)

It's common to hear semi-rude comments and questions about my work, especially from musicians. I'm getting better at being objective about these people. They're entitled to their opinions. I wish they could keep their thoughts to themselves, but hearing what they think is just the price you pay for being more visible. Or for being different.

One of my favorite sayings is, "Other peoples' opinion of me is none of my business." I should get that framed.

WHAT ADVICE WOULD YOU GIVE TO SOMEONE THAT WANTED TO HAVE A CAREER LIKE YOURS?

Big changes require sustained effort. Do something to forward your goal every single day. Maybe it's something small, like making a connection on LinkedIn or checking out a book from the library, but make progress a daily habit.

Also, quit thinking that progress requires money. So many entrepreneurs tell me, "I want to start my project, but I don't have enough money." Every time I ran out of money,

I asked myself, "Is there some work I can do on my project today that doesn't cost anything?" The answer was always "yes." You'll eventually find the money if it's important enough to you.

Once you've gotten things going, join some professional organizations. Go to networking events, conventions, etc. Try on this new role and see how it feels. You might realize you have as much right to be there as anyone else does.

IS THERE ANYTHING YOU WOULD LIKE TO ADD?

Music was hard for me because I was expected to shut out everything else. Other people assumed I wasn't focused if I had other hobbies. Now I realize that I wasn't the problem—varied interests make you smarter, more capable, and more creative. If musicians were encouraged to seek out diverse experiences, the field of classical music would be a better, healthier, more profitable one.

8

Creating a Teaching Career

Like so many young musicians, I was encouraged to get an education degree "as a backup." So when I didn't "make it" as an oboist, I could teach. I didn't want to teach; I was interested only in being an artist, a performer. My parents—initially—insisted.

My parents and I were both wrong, but not for the reasons any of us thought!

I started at the Eastman School of Music as a double major in performance and education. I took one education class. Not one semester of an education class, one class. I immediately knew that degree was not for me. That first session was an overview, and they laid out the curriculum the program would be following—instrumental methods, child development courses, student teaching—and they spoke with such pride and love about the profession of teaching.

I walked straight from that class to the registrar to drop the major.

I did not care for children. I did not want to lead a band or an orchestra. I only wanted to play in the orchestra, and it was perfectly apparent to me that the Ed Major was going to require a lot of tiresome non-oboe-playing time that would lead to a job I didn't want.

I have never once met a high school band director whose job I envied, though I know plenty of music teachers who love their work and are happy. But it is not the right job for me, and for this reason I'm fully satisfied with my decision not to do it.

It turns out, though, and this would have surprised my younger self, that teaching is one of my very favorite things to do. I love working with someone one-to-one to find a breakthrough, to find their way to ease and effortlessness. The creativity of teaching is deeply fun and inspiring. But I maintain that running a band program or teaching elementary music classes would not have suited me.

Teaching private lessons can indeed be rewarding, and it is completely possible to make a legitimate living as a musician doing primarily that. I have friends and colleagues who can barely keep up with demand. They teach 30 or more students every week, creating a fun and fulfilling studio culture—and they truly love what they are doing.

For many musicians—for me, at times—it can feel like the teaching subsidizes the playing. Sure, you can make a hundred or two hundred dollars playing a rehearsal, but by the time you drive there and work for two-and-a-half hours, you almost certainly could have made more in lesson fees.

As enjoyable as teaching is, though, it is absolutely *not* the same experience as sitting in the orchestra with your peers, doing the actual music-making that attracted you to the profession in the first place! Those two things are different. The way you choose to balance your time, your energy, and your money is up to you.

GETTING STARTED

The first student I taught came to my tiny apartment where I taught her in my tiny bedroom. I had her buy the same first book I learned from, and I didn't have any ideas to teach her beyond how to play the notes and rhythms. I was not gifted at teaching. She did not stay with me for long.

The second student I taught stayed in her own house. I met her there, and taught her in her bedroom. This was a legitimately terrible experience. Her home was more than an hour from mine (much more when traffic was bad) and she could not actually play the oboe. She couldn't hear intervals smaller than a minor third—literally. I'd sing or play notes to her and she couldn't tell me which ones were higher or lower. And her father, who apparently worked a night shift, was always in a bathrobe in the house. This lasted about a year and she quit. I was greatly relieved.

No one starts out knowing how to be a great teacher. But everyone has to start somewhere!

Working with this second student, I began to get inventive. I began to leave behind that one book I'd been taught from and create my own assignments. The problems this girl had were different from the ones I had at her age, and they required different solutions. I wrote out exercises for her. I had her sing. I brought her Beethoven's Fifth Symphony because she recognized it, and we worked through some of those minor thirds.

Our work was not successful, in terms of nurturing a future oboist, but it taught me a lot. The same thing doesn't work for everyone. In every case, the goal is music, the goal is artistry, the goal is facility. But the path is always different, and that's where the pleasure lies. It was here that the creativity I bring to my teaching was born.

I've taught hundreds of students now, from beginners to very advanced players. Students of mine have attended major music schools and won professional auditions. Others have gone on to successful careers as teachers, computer programmers, lawyers, doctors, using the work ethic, grit, and musician superpowers that they gained from their studies.

I've got my schtick down: I can talk about embouchure or fake fingerings or reed crows easily and in many different ways. But the pleasure, every time, is in looking for that *Aha!* that solves a problem for that one person, the one in front of me right now, whether the goal is to slur to a G or to bring the audition committee to tears.

It was a while before I began to get good students, and then a while before I began to get great students. What does that even mean?

There are not bad, good, and great people. There are people who are more or less natural at the oboe, but that doesn't really matter. There are people who are more or less coachable, which does.

To me, a great student is one who wants to get better, who comes in with a self-awareness about his or her own weaknesses, and challenges me to be ever more clear, specific, and present with them as we work. I love someone who comes in with their own ideas and interpretation, and forces me to engage with and rethink mine.

Since those first few kids, I've always had a fleet of private students who came to my house or to my campus studio. I've had a collection of adjunct positions in colleges and universities, some of which you may have heard of and some of which you may not.

I never sought a big tenure-track position. That is not where I ever wanted my career path to go. But I have taught and taught and taught.

THE TURNING POINT

It was March of 2019. I was sitting in the orchestra playing Johannes Brahms' Symphony No. 1.

My own taste leans towards new music, and music that tells a story, and music that has some good crunch and dissonance. None of these characteristics describe Brahms' First, but of all the overplayed warhorse symphonies out there, it's my absolute favorite.

I love the melodies, and the drive, and the passion. I love the timpani at the beginning and the horn and flute solos at the end. And the amazing string chorale, and the trombones' entrance, and every single moment of my oboe part.

I can forgive it for not being edgy. I've always said that if you have to write a symphony, you might as well write Brahms' No. 1. It's essentially perfect.

So there I was in the orchestra, having just played my favorite solo—the one in the fourth and final movement that has such momentum and heroism and yearning and beauty—when a very clear voice inside my head said, in words: *What is even the point of all this?*

It shocked me. I couldn't ignore a voice that clear and strong, but I hadn't expected it. There I was, sitting in my orchestra, playing principal oboe on my all-time favorite piece, led by a conductor I liked and respected, surrounded by my wonderful colleagues, and I was so clearly over it—*all*. What on earth did I have to be unhappy about? What was I telling myself?

Looking back at that week in my calendar, I can see why the 2019 version of me might have been more than a little burned out.

I had 15 students that week, in three different locations, two of which were over 30 miles from home. One of those colleges was in a different time zone. My schedule included a full recital, a solo showcase, and nine rehearsals and performances with my quintet and my orchestra.

My husband was working in Chicago every day, and my daughter had activities every afternoon that required transportation and coordination. I was wrangling babysitters, dinners, student schedules, and showing up as a performer multiple times a day.

This was not an unusual week. Having all of the orchestra services—rehearsals and concerts—in my home town was a bonus. But the look of that calendar, from my 2021 perspective, gives me hives.

This is what a successful two-musician family was doing, and had to do, all the time.

On the surface, things were fine. We were making our mortgage payments, we were showing up artistically, we were doing good work. I was still finding my flow inside the orchestra services, and inside the lessons, mostly.

But there was no flow in my life outside of those services, no margin. We were constantly tired, nothing felt easy, and I was dying inside. That clear, unignorable voice was telling me that this was all too much.

I had to make changes.

I loved teaching. I brought myself fully to every lesson. But at a certain point I had too many lessons every week, and the space between them wasn't enough to recharge.

Performing was my life. I brought my whole self to every concert, but sometimes I found myself distracted and unable to engage in rehearsals. I was giving great presentations at my recitals, but I didn't have the time or the white space to market them well, so I was out there giving it all for small audiences and minimal ticket sales.

Between all of the visible things on my calendar, I was running a six-figure reed business, which required me to sit at my desk for a couple of hours every day to stay on top of my orders and cost me 4-5 additional hours each week to ship them out. I loved everything I was doing but I couldn't keep it up, and I didn't dare to slow down because I didn't know how.

When you are a musician, you know that every paycheck is precious. Just because you feel too busy this week, that's no reason to assume you'll be able to make rent next month. The work comes in waves, and you take it when it's offered, because you don't know when the next gig will come. The waves pass.

At least, that's the mindset I had in early 2019. I felt lucky that I was making my living. I felt proud that we could pay our bills. But I was giving 2000 percent every month and there was nothing left.

I am a happy person. I'm always happy. But I needed my life to change, and I didn't know how to get there. I couldn't see a vision beyond the one I was living in. I didn't know what the future was going to look like. I knew that I needed some space to figure it out.

So that May I graduated two students at one of my adjunct colleges and then resigned from it. I graduated five seniors from my private studio. I kept one adjunct position because I had two very serious rising seniors that I needed to see through. This left me with four sophomores who might have continued coming to my home—

but I couldn't stomach it. I agonized for a little while about cutting them loose.

After all, they hadn't done anything wrong. They were good kids. We'd been working together for years. I had a relationship with their families. Why should I fire these perfectly nice people from my studio? My husband listened to me dithering for a while and then blew my mind with this reframing: "You aren't firing them," he said. "You're leaving the job of private teaching."

That felt better. I've left jobs. I've quit things before, and quitting was exactly the thing I needed. I felt sad. I apologized to my students. I recommended other teachers. But I quit the job I had made for myself and instantly dropped from 18 students every week to four.

I knew that the right amount of teaching for me was not zero, but I couldn't do it the way I had been doing it. I needed white space around me to develop clarity on how to change.

HOW TO CREATE A TEACHING STUDIO YOU LOVE

If you are just starting out—if you have not taught music lessons before—you will need to get your hands dirty and have some successes and failures before you really know what you are about. It is difficult to have a teaching philosophy, a system, a routine before you have taken a number of students through the process. You just don't know what you don't know.

But teaching is such a profoundly rewarding, creative task. It's also an immediate route to improving your own playing. When you hear your student struggling with something, even if that concept is easy for you, you have to create words around how to do it better. Or you have to find a clear way to demonstrate it.

Developing that clarity in your own playing—being clear enough in your ability and your intention so a less experienced player can really hear the difference—is a benefit to you. Using your words, and putting your own musical instincts, your right-brain genius, into your left-brain vocabulary for someone else to understand will help you, too. Over time, you will develop ways of talking about these concepts that are yours and yours alone.

I have caught myself struggling to find a place to breathe when I work on my own repertoire, and heard my own words in my head—"Exhale early, exhale often"—and remembered that the solution to my breathing issues are always to be found earlier in the piece. I have reminded myself that the oboe is allowed to be easy, and have lightened my approach and found success where previously there had been struggle. I've said these words to so many people they've begun to sink in for me as well!

When you teach private lessons, you will have people at different levels working on different challenges in their playing. You will become skilled at meeting these people right where they are each week and finding ways to ease them forward on their own path. You will begin to trust yourself to be able to help people, even if the problems they come in with are new to you.

Over time, you will begin to see and understand patterns in how people learn, how they progress. You will find that there are concepts people need to hear over and over again. You will find universal issues that they all struggle with. You will identify how *you* learn and what you care about and what feels most important for you to teach.

At a certain point, you may begin to feel burned out, tired of saying the same things over and over. You may feel that teaching is taking over your life. At this point, or maybe just a little before, you might feel that it's time to evolve your studio into something else that is better for you.

The traditional model of music lessons—a student comes every Tuesday at 4:15 PM and gives you money; you give them some knowledge; and you continue in this way until eternity—is a *fantastic* way to start out. It brings some money in the door for you right away. You can work with students at all different levels. And you can figure out where your genius lies. You can begin to identify the things you like to talk about, the problems you are good at solving, and the kinds of students you like to work with.

Even at this phase of music lessons, you should have some good solid policies in place that protect you. I liked to have lessons paid monthly, rather than weekly, and paid in advance.

You should have written policies in place around makeup lessons, cancellations, no-shows, and extras like sheet music or photocopies or reeds. If you treat your teaching studio like a business worthy of respect—even when you have only a few students—your students and their parents will treat you as a person worthy of respect.

Pricing is one of the hardest things for some people. If you are just out of school, just starting out, you may be tempted to set your prices very low. This makes some sense. But you can get locked in down there so easily, and feel unable to raise those prices even as your studio—and your talent for teaching—grows.

And this way lies burnout!

If you only think about your hour as being worth $50, you have to work a lot of hours to make a good living.

Teaching is intense, mentally challenging labor. I used to teach 7-10 students in a row on Mondays—and I was fried when I left at the end of the evening. We teachers bring 100% to every session, bring all of our empathy and all of our attention and presence and all of our backlog of knowledge, our 10,000 hours of mastering our craft, and our will to impart that to someone else. That's a lot to ask for $50 an hour!

HOW I TRANSFORMED MY STUDIO

After working for about six months in my new skeleton studio—one day a week, three hours only—I had some room in my schedule and in my head, so I found myself interested in expanding my teaching life again. But I needed it to be different this time around.

I thought about the kind of person I wanted to teach: motivated, interested, smart, and open to experimenting. Responsible and willing to put in the time to implement the things we discuss. Willing to disagree and challenge me to make me more thoughtful with my words. In a word: adults.

I thought about what kind of teaching I loved the most: first lessons, during which I can make a dramatic improvement by talking about a fundamental principle, like air or posture, or big picture planning; group classes, in which I can bounce off of the energy of the group and let one person's question inspire a riff that educates everyone.

I thought about the kinds of things I like to talk about: the philosophy behind our musical and technical choices; the physical approaches to the instrument that make it feel and seem easy; practice techniques that solve problems efficiently and free the artist inside.

I thought about wanting the experience to have a beginning, a middle, and an end, so we didn't get trapped inside the infinite spiral of lessons that never culminate. I knew I didn't want to get constantly derailed with reeds and mechanical issues. Although these are important things, I wanted to separate them out.

Ultimately, when I created The Invincible Oboist, that's exactly what I made. I created a 3-month experience with weekly group classes, weekly reed sessions, and monthly private lessons. I marketed it to adult amateurs. And I priced it high enough to encourage commitment from my participants and to allow me to love over-delivering to them.

I worked to make our group classes as interactive as possible. I strove to give them fantastic value in their private lessons. I developed our community bonds through a Facebook group. This has been immensely rewarding for all of us!

NOW YOU TRY

Whether you are an experienced teacher looking to change your studio structure and policies, or whether you are just starting out, it is valuable to think about how you want things to look.

JUST START

If you're just getting started with private lessons, my best advice is to do a lot of them. Ask local band directors if their students need private lessons. Ask local teachers of your instrument if they have overflow or could direct students they don't want to you. Don't be too picky; work with lots of people and figure out how to help them. Get familiar with the kinds of problems they have. Develop a variety of ways to solve those problems. And while you are doing this, *notice.*

GET CURIOUS

If you're already active as a teacher, *notice.*

What kind of students do you like to work with? What age, what level, what do all of your current favorite students have in common?

How do you like to teach? Do you prefer groups or one-to-one sessions? Do you want to have contact every week? Would you want to create and share video lessons, or do you prefer to deliver every session live? Might you build up a library of video lessons that you could later sell passively? Do you want to work in-person or virtually? What kind of teaching feels easiest and most fun to you?

What do you want to teach? Is it merely how to play the instrument, or is there some specific angle that lights you up? Do you want to focus on ways to warm up and use scales? Do you want to focus on performance nerves? Audition prep? Do you want to teach people to improvise? To play by ear? To analyze the musical theory behind all of their works?

What kinds of things do you find yourself saying to *everyone* when you teach? Could you make a training or a group session to cover that material in more depth?

What kinds of things do you always wish you could find the time to teach? Or the time to explore? Sometimes raising a conversation within a group will clarify an idea I'd only started to have.

PRICING IS IMPORTANT

How much do you want to charge? When you are starting out, it's good practice to stay within the normal range for your area. Don't dramatically undercut the other local teachers. This kind of price competition reduces the value of lessons for everyone and hurts the community of musicians. Instead of trying to compete on price, which is nothing more than a race to the bottom for everyone, think about how *your* teaching techniques and *your* method add value to the experience you provide. What do you bring to the table that other teachers do not? How can you justify a higher price point by creating a higher-value product?

Pricing can be triggering, I know. Think about the number of hours you will need to spend creating and delivering your material, and make sure you're compensated for those hours. More importantly, think about the value someone will get from learning what you have to offer! Think about the value to them of having your attention on their problems. Think about whether you are sharing this material in a group or one-to-one. It *should* cost a lot to have your full attention on them as you deliver your valuable knowledge.

It can help to have someone to brainstorm your offer with. When I first created *The Invincible Oboist,* I had a coach who pushed me away from the simple math of dollars for hours; who pointed out ways in which I could be both more efficient and more valuable; who teased apart the ways I could bundle services or separate them to be optional add-ons.

If all of your friends and colleagues teaching in the traditional way are complaining about their studios but not making changes, they are not your best brainstorming partners. Look for someone who can think outside the box with you.

GET CLEAR

Do you need to start over from scratch in creating your teaching studio or just evolve it a little at a time toward something that works better for you? It's up to you, of course. I've seen teachers hesitate to make dramatic changes to their existing studio, lest it upset the balance that already exists. As you think through this question, you are allowed to center your own needs. How is the current arrangement working for you?

There's a difference between creating a brand new teaching offer—as I did with my Invincible Oboist program—and pivoting your existing studio into something that suits you more. Inertia is a powerful force, and often your students, *and* their parents, will resist dramatic changes. It might require some real effort on your part to enroll them in your new idea. You might lose a few students as you make your changes.

That possibility can be frightening. What would you do if half of your students quit? Again, a session with a thinking partner or a coach can help you work through this moment of scarcity mindset panic.

It's not a terrible idea to play out an actual response to this hypothetical question. If you lost half your studio, could you pay rent? How much would your rates have to go up to compensate for, say, five students dropping out? The worst case scenario probably won't happen, but if you spent some time thinking through it, you might feel a lot better prepared.

But let me promise you. Whether you decide to gradually evolve your teaching by leaning toward the changes you want, or whether you take the burn-it-all-down approach that I needed, there can certainly be a better version on the other side. If you take the time to think about it and to map out what you want it to look like, there will be a way to get it there.

As you create your path and your portfolio career, it's possible that some of the things you try will be missteps. This is normal! But on the whole, wouldn't you rather have tried and failed than not tried at all?

I don't think anyone reaches the pinnacle of success without some failures along the way. I've been telling a curated version of my story, trying to keep it as linear as possible. In the next chapter, I'll talk a little about some attempts I made to build things that didn't work out—and what I *learned* from each!

SPOTLIGHT ON A CAREER

JESSICA WILKINS

Jessica Wilkins is a multifaceted musician with a diverse oboe performance and composition career.

Composing and arranging are significant elements of Jessica's career. At age 18, she had a collection of her oboe duets published by RDG Woodwinds. By age 21, she had launched her online sheet music company (JDW Sheet Music) to showcase her original transcriptions. Her arrangements have been performed by solo artists and chamber music groups like Nancy Ambrose King, Cordancia Chamber Orchestra, University of Northern Colorado oboe studio, and Bocal Majority. Jessica is currently working on adding more music by underrepresented composers and educating the arts community on these composers' achievements through her Black Excellence Music Project.

Jessica lives in Los Angeles, CA where she is an active freelance oboist and teacher. As an oboist, Jessica has had the opportunity to perform throughout Southern California in recording sessions, orchestras, operas, and small chamber ensembles. She maintains a small private oboe studio, and has also been an active mentor to the students of the Inner City Youth Orchestra, which aims to bring high-quality music education to kids in low-income neighborhoods.

JESSICA, HOW WOULD YOU DESCRIBE YOUR CURRENT WORK?

Oboist/teacher/sheet music publisher.

HOW DID YOU START DOING WHAT YOU DO?

I started arranging in high school for myself and my friends. We didn't have money for music so I would make arrangements from piano scores I owned. After undergrad, I launched JDW Sheet Music in 2013 to showcase my work.

WHAT DO YOU LOVE ABOUT YOUR WORK?

I love hearing my music performed around the world.

WHAT IS THE MOST CHALLENGING ASPECT OF IT FOR YOU?

Dealing with the legal and tax aspects of running a business since I don't come from a legal or tax background.

WHAT BARRIERS DID YOU HAVE TO OVERCOME TO GET TO WHERE YOU ARE?

Since I started my business at a young age, a lot of people wrote me off for my inexperience. I had to prove to people that I was a legitimate business.

WHAT ADVICE WOULD YOU GIVE TO SOMEONE WHO WANTED TO HAVE A CAREER LIKE YOURS?

Get started even if you're not 100% ready. Taking risks is scary, but the reward is worth it.

9

Failures

ot everything I create works.

MUSICIANS FOR MICHIANA

My first big failure was my chamber music series: *Musicians for Michiana*. Why do I consider this a failure?

The concept was all right. Local classical musicians created themed concerts which featured living composers. Each concert was a partnership with a local non-profit. They brought their audience to us, and we brought ours to them. The non-profits got to speak at the event, and the audience donated to them on a pay-what-you-can basis.

I partnered with a local music school that sponsored our grant applications and supported me in navigating the start-up process in exchange for one dedicated concert each season. We had three seasons with four concerts each, but I elected not to go forward with the project.

It turned out that once we had the basic structure created, there were things I definitely enjoyed about the process. I loved presenting the concerts, of course. I didn't perform in all of them but I did in most, and performance is always my happy place. I enjoyed meeting representatives of various non-profits throughout the city, learning more about their organizations, and helping to raise money for them.

But the business model just wouldn't work. My concept was to donate ticket proceeds directly to the non-profits, while I raised money to pay the musicians. I crowdfunded the first season, hustling like crazy to make our Indiegogo go. We applied for and received a grant to run the second season, but I self-funded a shoestring third season and it felt anticlimactic.

In retrospect, if I'd started early on to create a real 501(C)(3) organization, I might have had the paperwork together by the time that local music school changed management, and I might have had a team of people to help me. But that also would have locked me into continuing!

Really, what I learned was that I did not like asking for money. I didn't mind seeking donations for those terrific local organizations, but asking for money for my own series was absolutely no fun. I didn't want anyone to have a hold over me. I didn't like the tedious work of applying for grants. I didn't like the bookkeeping. And over that time, I learned that those are the basic fundamental tasks of a non-profit. (Should I have known that before I started? Yes. Did my conservatory education teach me *anything* about this? No.)

For me, it feels easier, more nimble, and more fun to put together recitals on my own, without the baggage of checking in with partners and confirming with organizations. I can come up with a fun program, get on the phone to a few venues, and make something happen very fast. I can sell tickets or I can pitch to a presenter who has a budget. I can collaborate with my colleagues to market and promote it, and I can design another program next month if I like. The additional effort of involving others, planning a full season in advance, and raising money is not my cup of tea. I'd rather pay collaborators out of my pocket so I can maintain control. I didn't know this before I started Musicians for Michiana. Now I do.

But I also understand now that if you want to create something that will outlive you, you have to enroll more people in the effort. When I got busy and distracted after the third season of MFM, there was no one else to take the reins and do any of the work I had been doing. I had been so sure I could do everything myself that no one else was involved, so the whole project depended on me to keep it going—and I didn't want to.

Through this process, I got a lot of clarity about how I like to work and how I don't. I learned a lot about how to do this better next time—if I wanted to. I learned about grant-writing, which served me well when a later grant I wrote covered some of the costs of producing my CD and when an Indiana Arts Commission grant paid in part for a piece I commissioned.

I became a lot more comfortable having live meetings with people and speaking about my vision. I grew to love enrollment conversations and the process of getting people on my side. I built a tiny but very enthusiastic audience of people who continued to follow me through future performances. Musicians for Michiana was a flop, but it was a fun flop.

What if, in the process of your evolution, it's not really a problem to try things out and decide they're not for you?

CRUX FINDER TAROT

I'm a musician, but I'm also a creative and intuitive person, and sometimes that other side of me wants to come forward.

I have always loved the Tarot. These 78 cards express the range of human experience. They have history and imagery and beauty. They've been explored by a thousand different artists, and they have both an air of mystery and a hint of naughtiness to them. After spending a few years reading for friends and doing free online readings through someone else's platform, I decided that I was ready to come out and officially be a Tarot weirdo.

This felt terribly vulnerable to me. All of my earned visibility was around the oboe. What would people think if I started down this strange and unconventional path? Would I lose the respect of my colleagues who expected me to be both sensible and oboe-focused? Would I lose customers? Who wants to buy reeds from someone who has an interest besides reeds? Would people hate me?

This sensitivity around my Tarot visibility sounds silly, but it was a real concern for me as I began to share my work and thoughts. The fear couldn't stop me, though; I felt a creativity within me that had to come out.

I had found the Tarot to be a great source of *flow*. I loved tapping into that intuitive place and how the words would come through me when I found it. I will chase that flow feeling wherever it leads me, and I felt called to do more Tarot readings. Plus, I'm entrepreneurial through and through, and saw an opportunity to monetize a passion.

I started by creating a Facebook page and committing to a posting schedule. Every weekend I would draw two cards for the week, write substantially on them, and share. I would do a Card Of the Day on Monday, Wednesday, and Friday: drawing it, photographing it, and writing a brief uplifting message. I told stories on Tuesday and Thursday about my own Tarot journey, about the history of the cards, or whatever I was thinking about.

I did most of this writing over the weekend and scheduled the posts out so I didn't feel the stress of having to make a new idea every day! I was organized, and I did love writing and cards, so this didn't feel too onerous.

I also created a small menu of offerings: small email readings for a small fee, larger ones for a larger fee. I made a new gmail address with my tarot name. I connected that email to a PayPal account. My idea was that it looked a little more professional to invoice and communicate through a branded email, and that I might not have to use my name so publicly.

Getting this all started was a real visibility journey. I started that Facebook page, made it public, but didn't actually announce it at first, relying on friends and algorithms to bring in traffic. I included a photo of myself turned away, with my face behind cards.

I took the steps that were a tiny bit out of my comfort zone at first, and gradually became more open. This is not the fastest way to claim your place in a field, but it felt safe enough and comfortable enough to me. It's OK to take your time and to lean into the things that feel easy and fun, or at least only minimally challenging.

I ran this page for about seven months. I really enjoyed it. By the end I had around 150 followers, and I had good engagement on my posts, and I was perfectly comfortable being open about that side business. I sold maybe ten readings altogether, and enjoyed delivering them. It wasn't exactly profitable, but it was an interesting creative outlet and I liked it.

And then it was summer and I didn't feel like it anymore. The fun of my Tarot business had run its course. As the fall rolled around and I got busier again, I let the page go fallow.

In one very real sense, this was a business failure. I put in seven months of effort, never got profitable or highly visible, and quit when I got bored. But in another sense, it was a perfect learning experience for me. And probably for all of us.

Because here's what *really* happened: I felt a calling and I created a minimum viable offering—I didn't build a website, I didn't make business cards, I didn't hire a staff. If this had taken off and I had felt my passion continuing, I could have done some of that in the second year. But what I needed to do was take action and start, feel what it would be like to do this thing, and make it visible so I could see if anyone liked it or wanted it.

I have seen people dither and struggle over starting a new venture. I have seen them hold off until the offer is perfect, until they have their site and processes in place. I have seen them pay for logo design long before they have a business.

I could have built out the entire structure before I started, but how bad would it have felt seven months later when I decided not to continue? What a lot of wasted effort! I wanted to see if this would work, if people would be interested, if I would enjoy it. So I started, and I evolved, and when I had the information I needed, I decided to quit and I broke even.

This business was not yet profitable, but it was on a good trajectory and none of the aspects of it felt difficult or stressful to deliver. I could have gotten there. I chose not to.

The other lasting benefit of this experience manifested in the rest of my content. After I left the tarot page behind, I began to share some tarot writing as a semi-regular part of my profile. I really loved the opportunity to share messages of positivity and good practical advice, and I loved having my audience see me as a more complete person, not exclusively oboe-focused. Without meaning to, I happened upon a valuable lesson about being unique online.

There's a lot of noise in online marketing. There are a lot of oboists, a lot of reed businesses, a lot of people showing up to market one thing or another. But I was that oboist who also read Tarot. I was that oboist who was an expert in something else. I was that oboist who had a characteristic quirky writing style.

These qualities made me memorable. They improved my overall visibility, and they grew my business. People still occasionally reach out to me for tarot advice, and I love responding. Social media should be social, and I love when it is.

Crux Finder Tarot was an experiment that failed, but one that taught me a lot. That's what experiments are for!

REEDING CIRCLES

I wanted groups of oboists learning together. I wanted to have the exciting group energy I remembered from the Eastman School of Music, where my colleagues were amazing humans and musicians who made me want to sound better, want to *be* better, people with whom I could celebrate and mourn when things went a certain way.

I had had hints of this kind of group energy at my annual Oboe Reed Boot Camp, where a room full of mostly adult oboists bonded over the difficulty of crafting these tiny pieces of damp wood, and became friends and laughed together and learned together for two straight days.

The offer I tried to create was called a *Reeding Circle.* I wanted it to be a social reed making work time that a group of people could do together, with my support. I wanted people to become friends and love showing up.

That's what I wanted. But geography is a challenge for oboists. It's rare to have more than a few players in any given town. And at that, they are apt to be at very different levels, needing different things. It's one thing to get people to come to South Bend for a long weekend of oboe celebration once a year. It is quite another to propose that they commute here for an hour and a half once a month.

While my teaching studio was large, these groups had a moderately successful couple of years. I would host Reeding Circles twice a month, at two different universities, free to my students and open to the public for a small fee. There were enough students who wanted reed help, and occasionally we'd welcome a vaguely interested follower from outside of my immediate teaching studio.

But as my studio shrank—first, by attrition and then, by my pivot —it became more and more difficult to sustain this process. By the end, I was hosting one circle a month, at my house, and there was often only one person there. And she was getting a discount anyway.

This was not a success, and I was struggling to decide how to end it when COVID hit. On the plus side, the coronavirus made a clear cut ending to my limping Reeding Circles. On the minus side, you know, an enormous global pandemic shut all of the world's stages down, and claimed millions of lives.

But as I was working on my various pivots, creating programs, it became clear that geography was no longer a problem for oboists, or for anyone. The world was connected online now in a way that had not existed before. And people were lonely in their houses, with time on their hands.

I found that people *wanted* to get together and make reeds and chat, so I invented *Reed Club.* It has been through a few iterations in terms of pricing, schedule, and format, but we've settled it into being a regular Monday night meetup, with a recurring monthly fee. People come and go, but we have enough regulars to keep a friendly culture alive, and everyone's reeds are improving and everyone feels less alone!

In terms of my own business, this program makes a ton of sense. It's the least expensive way for people to work with me, so it really invites people in to try out the culture I'm creating. It is valuable for me as an add-on or bundle. It's an integral part of my Invincible Oboist program. I can offer it to people who want to take a few lessons—a monthly bundle of bi-weekly lessons and Reed Club is a terrific value for them and less effort for me to deliver than weekly sessions in which we have to spend time dealing with reeds one-on-one.

And, finally, I feel like I have a college reed room culture to play in. Sometimes I lecture or demonstrate in Reed Club, sometimes we talk about reed making philosophy, sometimes we take questions and focus on individual people's individual reeds, sometimes we break out into rooms so we can just chat.

What is the lesson for us here? Reeding Circles were a failure because of logistics and geography. When those issues were solved, by the internet and a pandemic, Reed Club was able to take off and thrive. The idea that I had, of creating connections and community among oboists, was worth holding onto, was worth my perseverance.

Is it possible that sitting down and brainstorming solutions could have brought me to a better version of this sooner? Absolutely. I've learned lately that a ten-minute thinking session can produce a lot of brilliance and productivity, but it was always a struggle for me to focus like that when I was busy all the time. I need white space on my calendar and a little bit of boredom for inspiration to strike, and then I need a minute to actually think about it.

Is this by any chance true for you, too?

NOW YOU TRY

If what you are working on is not working out, that's OK. Not everything is great the first time, and a failure—or a lack of immediate success—doesn't define your career or your life. If you try something and it turns out to not be a fit for you, you are not stuck in it forever.

So take a look. What in your life isn't working as well as you'd like? What is the thing that, every time you think about it, you sigh and grit your teeth a little? What is the thing that you secretly wish another pandemic would remove from your life? Maybe you're not calling it a failure; sometimes it takes distance to identify those! Maybe it's just something that isn't giving you what you had hoped it would.

Is it possible that a little brainstorming could yield a possible solution, one that doesn't require as dramatic a gesture as the Coronavirus lockdown? What would make that annoyance 5% better? Would that be better enough? What could improve the energy around it? What could fix it entirely?

Plenty of people let the fear of failure hold them back. They dream up ideas and then they delay until those ideas get created by others or until the urge passes. I'd love to see you try your bold idea before you give up on it!

What have you been hesitating to start? What's kicking around in the back of your mind? What's a thing you'd like to share with the world and haven't yet? What might it look like to have a minimum viable offer, or even just to have an idea that you share openly? What is holding you back? What are you afraid of, actually?

If you knew you could not fail, or if you knew that failure was just one short-term step along your growth path, what would you create?

10

Making Intentional Choices

Most musicians understand that their musical career won't start immediately after they graduate. Almost no one gets a big job straight out of school, no matter how excellent that early training was. The opportunities are just too few.

Recent graduates expect to have some sort of day job, some sort of dues-paying time when they are playing in a training orchestra, a community orchestra, or not at all. They expect to hustle for playing work and take auditions and teach the hand-me-down students other teachers pass along. And they are willing to wait and mark time for a while. A career isn't built overnight.

That said, getting started in the world is hard for everyone! When you are setting up your first apartment, when you are living off the paycheck from your first job, when you are trying to navigate car registration and student loan payments and rent and roommates, the whole thing can feel overwhelming, and that's totally aside from the development of your creative career! So it's unsurprising that many young musicians kind of camp out in their lives for a little while. Multiple roommates, hand-me-down furniture, a day job, scattered gigs, and credit cards to cover the gaps. I know that's what things looked like for me!

After all, if the next audition could uproot you and move you across the country *and* completely change your economic situation, why should you worry about furnishing your home or paying off your debts now? The very next time you get onto an audition stage, that ten minutes in the spotlight could change your entire life. Why worry about the money today? And why think about putting roots down where you are? Why look for a life partner before you settle in the amazing city that is going to be your final destination? There's plenty of time, isn't there?

Well... There is and there isn't. But while you are waiting, every day is an actual part of your life, right? Every day that goes by is an opportunity to build your life, and your life is a thing that is happening right now. You should keep sending out resumes and taking auditions if you want, you should keep looking ahead to the future, but you should pay attention to building the life and the career you have around you right now, too. If that big job happens, there's plenty of time to find your way there, but meanwhile, you are allowed to make choices for yourself. You are allowed to take agency in your own life.

MY STORY

When I graduated from Eastman, I moved with my then-boyfriend to Chicago. We had both won positions in the Civic Orchestra of Chicago, the Chicago Symphony's training orchestra, and that was a huge stroke of luck. It's not always easy for couples who are both performers to wind up in the same place. Auditions can be such a randomizing factor.

At that time, that orchestra paid something like $2,000 a year. *A. Year.* It was never designed to be a real job, just a supplement to your education. What it gave us, though, was two years of valuable musical training and a reason to be in Chicago, where we were able to make contacts and begin to freelance.

We played in that group and lived together in a series of very small, very silly shared housing situations for about a year and a half while we both took auditions. Then we decided that it was time to take some agency.

We weren't going to wait for a job to pull us apart, we were going to get married, and we did. We figured that as our careers developed, as we were invited to other places, as we made choices, we would make them together, and that has proved to be the case.

A marriage between two musicians without jobs is an economically questionable idea, right? We would have been more financially comfortable faster if either of us had been less committed to the art, the craft, the lifestyle of music. One spouse with a salaried job and health insurance would have made things much easier—but there's a tradeoff to consider there, too. When one partner is tied to a place and a company and a paycheck, the other has less flexibility to take auditions or to accept work that is far away. The cost of moving is greater. You can't just tear someone out of their good job that they like so you can accept a $24,000 a year position somewhere else. The tradeoff for stability now can be a lack of flexibility later.

Let's add that the partner who is making the money might have some desires as well. Might want the musician partner to contribute equally. Might want the musician partner to be available to hang out on weekends and evenings. Might expect that the musician partner will want to settle down and have children even before getting the job she wants.

Steve and I understood each other. We knew that we were talented, that we loved what we were doing, that we wanted to work in music much more than we wanted nice things. We knew that we were willing to wait for "grown-up" life to start, and it was more fun to wait together. And we enjoyed our 20s living in Chicago and growing our networks and making friends and taking auditions.

As we entered our 30s, though, still in Chicago, we began to get a teeny bit impatient. Scraping together a living was all very well and good, but some of our friends had houses. People our age had investments. People our age had cars that didn't have to be held together with duct tape.

I didn't mind the leanness so much, but it felt disempowering to be still waiting, hoping to be chosen by a big employer. It felt bad to be marking time in a small apartment, aware that this might not be our real life even yet. It felt like we weren't committing to the life we actually had while we were waiting for the life we wanted, and that lack of commitment began to feel unacceptable.

So we decided. It felt so good to decide.

We were living in Chicago, we were freelancing in the city and had small contracts in regional orchestras outside of it. We had friends, we had a network. This was a place we could live. We bought a condo. It felt so good to decide.

The fact that this condo, purchased at the peak of the real estate bubble, proved to be an objectively poor financial decision does not take away from my larger message, which is that you are allowed to make choices that feel right for you. You don't have to wait to be chosen. You can choose yourself and assert that the place you are living is a place you want to commit to. You can decide to build a life where you are, instead of continuing to hope for an outside force to act upon you (an audition, a university job offer, etc). And if later on, you change your mind? You are allowed to do that, too.

A few years later I won my principal oboe job in the South Bend Symphony. This was just another small regional orchestra a long way from home, but this one was a tipping point. At that time, I had an adjunct teaching position at Valparaiso University in Indiana. I had a position in the Northwest Indiana Symphony. When I added the South Bend schedule to my calendar, it turned out that every single week I had to make at least one trip to Indiana, and more often three to five trips. Our condo was on the far north side of Chicago, which meant I spent a minimum of an hour grinding through city traffic before I could even start to drive the required Indiana miles.

I have no passion for Indiana as a state. It's too conservative, too backward, too rural. We loved our life in Chicago. But our expensive little box of a condo, with people above us, below us, and on each side, was sapping all of our money. And the commute—90 minutes to three hours every day, each way—was awful. And let's be honest here: South Bend is a nice town with a *very low* cost of living.

So the next big decision we made was to move. We rented a three bedroom house, walking distance from the hall, walking distance to the river, walking distance to the pub. It cost us less than half what our monthly condo payments had. We discovered that our health insurance premiums went down when we moved, and our car insurance, too. Groceries were substantially cheaper. It was much less expensive to live after we moved out of the big city!

We could commute back to Chicago for gigs, and the bulk of that driving was easy highway miles. We maintained our contacts there and cultivated new connections with the arts groups nearby. After all, we were in a city with an orchestra and a big university, within easy driving distance of eight or ten other small orchestras in Michigan and Indiana. When I went from being one of a hundred oboists in town to being one of two or three, my teaching studio grew very fast, and I was highly in demand as a teacher, coach, and performer. Steve found the same, as a bassoonist, conductor, and composer. The opportunities were easier to harness in our new smaller city. South Bend proved to be ideal.

The next bit of this story might feel predictable. We decided to have a child. I was in my mid-30s and did not particularly care for babies, but the biological clock is a powerful thing. It is notable that this decision came only after we moved and stabilized our finances. I don't know that I ever would have considered this if we were still scrambling to make payments in Chicago, commuting hours and hours every day through traffic. But we felt secure and relaxed in our rented house in Indiana, and had the breathing room to consider our options. We chose to go for it.

This is important. No one has to have a child. It is not an inevitable life choice. I don't have any agenda about this on your behalf. You could choose to have zero children or seven. But making that decision for yourself is a grown-up, human choice that you are allowed to make as a grown-up human, regardless of whether you have gotten a big job yet or not. You should certainly consider your economic situation and the time commitments you and your partner have. And you should make the choice that is right for you, when you choose to.

Steve and I were so lucky to have each other as partners when we started down this path. Children are expensive. We were not wealthy. But the magical thing about being two working musicians is that we both had a lot of time at home. I could teach students in my studio with a baby. I could make reeds. Steve could watch her when I went to evening rehearsals. We juggled our schedules and hired babysitters when we had to, but our daughter had a parent with her most of the time. We never had to send her to daycare, which was fortunate for our wallets. Sometimes the logistics got complicated, but we always worked it out. If we had been in a different situation—if one of us was working full-time for someone else, instead of for ourselves—it would have been differently challenging.

Nearly twelve years later, I can attest to how difficult it was to have a baby and then a toddler while simultaneously building a career; how difficult it is to juggle my schedule and my desires with those of two other people in my nuclear family. I can also attest to the joy that's come from it, and I wouldn't change a thing.

AFTER ZOE

It was after my daughter was born that I began to blog. It was after my daughter was born that I realized I could put more energy into my reed business—*and make it a business,* not just extra pocket money.

It was after my daughter was born that I began to experiment with group classes. I invented Oboe Reed Boot Camp to use my time more efficiently, bring in more money, and create more stability in my life and bank account.

In retrospect, I realize that I had sown the seeds of my portfolio career in my mid-20s. But it wasn't until I was 35 and a mother that I got intentional and leaned into the greatness that is my current life.

When I had my daughter, I had to change my pacing. Before Zoe, everything I was doing was about the oboe. I lived to improve my playing, one practice session, one mock audition, one gig at a time.

After Zoe, I didn't know who I was anymore.

The emotional transition to parenthood—to putting the needs of a helpless person above mine—was enormous. No more so for me than for anyone else, I'm sure; bringing another human into the world and assuming responsibility for its life is a huge change.

I was accustomed to being the most important person in my own life, and when I wasn't anymore it was difficult. My identity as a musician had to make room for my identity as a mother. My body changed, my brain changed, and my life changed.

During this time, I started my blog. I was desperate for a creative outlet in the months after Zoe was born. It was summer and I'd intentionally taken time off to adjust to motherhood. But I was so bored.

Zoe was enchanting. I adored her, I played with her. But babies sleep all the time and their needs are repetitive. I wasn't working in an orchestra, and I was bored. So I wrote.

This was the first time I ever considered myself anything more than an oboist.

Writing is so much a part of my identity today that I'm surprised when I realize I didn't used to do it. Sharing my thoughts with the world felt vulnerable at first; now it's so natural I feel antsy when I don't have time to put my thoughts on paper. I practice every day, but I also type every day. I now consider myself a communicator first and foremost—in writing, in teaching, coaching, and speaking, *and* through the oboe—a musician with a point of view, rather than an oboist who can play the oboe. This change *all* happened after Zoe.

REAL ESTATE

There's another interlude of adulting to talk about at this point: after a few years of renting, we decided to buy a house. Were we wildly committed to our life in Indiana? No, I was still taking auditions and we were still open to the idea of moving if anything came up. But the recovery from the Great Recession was slow to arrive in South Bend, and in that fact we saw an opportunity.

We bought a tiny foreclosed home in a kind-of-okay neighborhood. Really, the house was barely this side of inhabitable. But it was so cheap that we bought it outright with the change we scraped up from under the sofa cushions. More accurately, we maxed out two credit cards and borrowed eight thousand dollars from my mom, and just like that, we had a house. We lived in it with no mortgage and paid off the cards and the family within a year. Steve fixed it up by watching DIY videos and experimenting. We painted it and we sold it for a 50% profit a few years later and purchased the big old house that we now live in and love.

This period of our life wasn't all fun and games. It stunk to be living in a crummy little house with one room after another stripped down to the joists. I was always a little embarrassed when students came over for their lessons. Our neighbors were... characters. We were in our late 30s and didn't feel great about our home. I tell this story, though, because it is a part of our path to the present day, and because things certainly weren't all bad. We had good times, we laughed, we hosted parties, and my daughter grew from a toddler to a kindergartner. You can enjoy your life no matter the circumstances, and you can be in a weird place on the way to better things.

The path I describe here is specific to me, and specific to the time and place we were in. You can't count on being able to afford a rickety little house in just any city at any time, but there are still some useful takeaways here.

NOW YOU TRY

If you're just beginning to build your portfolio career, you might find yourself in a place where you are waiting: waiting to be hired, waiting to hear from contractors, waiting to see what your work schedule will be, waiting for the next big thing to happen. You may feel like your life is not your own, like you serve at the whim of the wider world. To an extent, that is true. You can't just *decide* to work every week in an orchestra, you can't just *decide* to be a top-ranked freelancer, you can't just *decide* to have a thriving teaching studio. These things take time; you can't control as much as you would wish.

But you can decide to take more action than simply clicking refresh in your email inbox every five minutes and hoping.

JUST START

If you are not getting the opportunities you want, can you actively make more connections? Can you reach out to more musicians and play for them? Can you do a little of that every month?

If you aren't getting the students you want, can you visit band programs and youth orchestras and talk to the kids? Can you volunteer to do some sectionals and make yourself super helpful to the players? Can you create educational, enjoyable content that speaks to the audience you want to reach, and share it on platforms where your people are? Can you put together a weekend workshop that speaks to their pain point, and sell lessons from there?

Even if you are struggling to make ends meet, can you make some life decisions for yourself?

It's so tempting to just keep waiting. This audition went pretty well, no doubt the next one will go better, so let me just keep doing what I'm doing. I'll practice. I'll scrape together the rent for another month. And I won't think too hard about the big picture.

But let me ask you. What are you waiting for? Seriously.

GET CLEAR

If you complete the sentence, "I can't wait until __________, so I can finally __________," what comes up for you?

"I wish __________ would happen so I can start to __________," is another promising path to your truth.

Do you have an agenda for your life, and are there a lot of "if __________, then __________," statements in it?

You don't have to blindly leap forward right this minute; you don't have to have a relationship or a baby or a mortgage before you're ready. But if you feel like you are in a holding pattern, just waiting for your turn to shine; waiting for your real life to start and hoping it's coming just around the corner; I would encourage you to explore ways you might take agency yourself to move toward the life you want.

What if you let yourself shine now?

The place you are living now, the work you are doing—do you love it? What about it do you love? What's not working well for you?

Is there a decision to be made, one you're putting off? Is it possible that just making that decision will give you permission to move forward and own your life and career?

Is the thing you are waiting for—the audition win, the freelance call, the magical day when your entire income is based on performance or teaching—still a thing you genuinely want? If not, you are allowed to change your mind. Even if you've been fixated on being a musician ever since middle school, you might find that the 26-, 36-, 46-year-old you feels differently.

You don't have to be held captive by the decisions of a child. If you find yourself enjoying your side hustle or your day job, and you want to lean into that and out of the hustle of the gig scene, you can. If you find that the condo you bought was a mistake, you can sell it or rent it. If you want to rebalance your portfolio career, you can do that, too.

And on the other hand, if that thing you are waiting for is still worth waiting for, then by all means wait! Keep working toward the end goal! Just know that there's no shame in simultaneously building your studio, your business, your relationships, your wealth. Your life is happening right now and you are allowed to commit to it, in whatever way you need that to look.

SPOTLIGHT ON A CAREER

SEAN MCNEELY

Sean has had a diverse and accomplished career both as a musician and as a tax preparer. As an orchestral musician, he has performed as a clarinetist with the Chicago Symphony Orchestra and New York Philharmonic among other groups. He was also a Grand Prize winner of the Fischoff National Chamber Music Competition in 2002.

Sean is an active theater musician, playing all the clarinets, flutes, saxes, and even oboe for productions in the Chicagoland area. This includes several pre-Broadway runs with the original stars, long term sit-down runs of *Wicked* and *Jersey Boys*, as well as countless regional productions.

Ten years ago, Sean became a tax preparer. He passed the three-part IRS special enrollment exam and became an Enrolled Agent (EA) in 2014. The EA credential is the highest credential offered by the IRS. He currently runs his own tax preparation business while still actively performing.

SEAN, HOW WOULD YOU DESCRIBE YOUR CURRENT WORK?

Freelance performing musician (orchestral sub/theater woodwind doubler), theater orchestra contractor, tax return preparer operating my own business.

HOW DID YOU START DOING WHAT YOU DO?

Mid-freelance career, I felt the need to take some control over my own destiny. As a freelancer, I would get hired at the whim of others. I wanted a piece of my career that I had complete control over. After testing some options, I found my way into tax preparation. The fact that it is completely outside the traditional musical world actually appealed to me. It satisfied a part of my brain that performing never could.

WHAT DO YOU LOVE ABOUT YOUR WORK?

Tax preparation has an aspect of helping other people. I'm able to guide them through a process they might not understand and/or are fearful of. The gratitude I receive from clients is very rewarding. It's also very enlightening to get an insight on how others live. I cannot deny that I've always liked numbers. Getting to use numbers beyond 1, 2, 3, and 4 is good for me.

WHAT IS THE MOST CHALLENGING ASPECT OF IT FOR YOU?

Time management! Keeping up my instrumental skills while keeping up with clients and the latest tax law changes can get very challenging, especially during tax season. I always have to remember to leave some "me" time during the busy periods as well.

WHAT BARRIERS DID YOU HAVE TO OVERCOME TO GET TO WHERE YOU ARE?

Starting a second career and more importantly my own business seemed daunting. It's one thing to work for someone else, but to create and start your own business is a whole other ballgame. I had to trust in myself, and believe I could run an actual business as opposed to just being an employee of one. And also realize that if I didn't succeed, that it didn't make me a failure.

WHAT ADVICE WOULD YOU GIVE TO SOMEONE WHO WANTED TO HAVE A CAREER LIKE YOURS?

Figure out your own game plan. What are your goals? What will make you happy? Not just financially, but emotionally/personally too. Define that first, then develop a strategy to get you there. Don't be afraid to revisit and revise those goals and strategies often as well.

PART THREE
Now You Try

When I had that moment of shocking clarity in the middle of Brahms First, I realized just how burned out I was. I needed a pivot. I needed a change. The life I'd been building wasn't working for me anymore.

The changes I made weren't dramatic: I moved from teaching weekly lessons to teaching group programs, but that's still teaching. I moved from writing occasionally to writing all the time, but that's still writing.

What I really did was take a step back to look at where I was and what I needed, and then I leaned into the changes I imagined. It was basically easy, because I'd been building my portfolio career for years. I just didn't have the intentionality behind it that I do now.

Let me say this again: once I got clear on what I needed, it was relatively easy to make it happen.

The foundations of my career were already in place. I had some visibility and platforms that I was already using to communicate with my audience. I had the teaching skills, the performance skills, the website infrastructure in place.

What I didn't have was a framework for zooming out, looking at the big picture, and thinking about where I wanted to go. What I didn't have was a coach helping me flesh out my ideas. And in the absence of a vision, I had unintentionally evolved toward being busier and busier until I couldn't do it any more.

In these next chapters, I'd like to walk you through some concrete steps toward identifying your own vision, seeing your own path, and putting infrastructure in place so you are ready for your own big moves and ready to be *The Happiest Musician.*

11

The First Steps

I've talked a lot about my entrepreneurial and artistic journey so far, and I can only reiterate how much fun I've been having with it. Sometimes, is work just work? Sure. Sometimes I show up for a gig I don't love, sometimes I don't feel like teaching, certainly I don't always want to create a new video or even think about the oboe.

But I adore my career and my life. I love the flexibility, the creative freedom, the income, the community. I feel a sense of purpose when I help people past the struggle, whether as musicians or in their own creative career pivots.

Maybe, though, when you picture your ideal life, it's not like mine. Maybe the thought of creating frequent written and video content sounds awful. Maybe you don't aspire to a solo career, however self-made. Maybe your passion is for the technology of music. Maybe you want to make a difference in the way orchestral auditions happen. Maybe you want to tour the country reading your poetry in coffee shops. Maybe you want to start a wildly successful podcast interviewing farmers. The idea that lights you up is what you should pursue!

This is where you start to build that path.

In this chapter, you will create your vision. You will imagine what your version of a successful, abundant career and life will look like, and you'll dream up the details with clarity and commitment. This will take time; it's a process of continuing evolution. You may reimagine this vision for yourself a couple of times a year, allowing it to change and grow along with you.

MAKE THE FUTURE MANAGEABLE

Set your vision in the manageably distant future: not ten years off because who even knows what that might look like; and not next month because you probably can't create major change by then. Start with something between six months and three years away. As you build your vision, allow yourself to balance what you believe to be realistic and achievable with what you think of as amazing and aspirational. Enough truth to seem possible, enough fantasy to excite you.

Just having a vision of how you want your life to look is not enough, right? You have to work for it and move toward it actively. But life is not linear. It's not always obvious in the moment what choice is strategically best. It's not always apparent what to do. If it were, this would be easy.

As you are looking at choices in real time, though, as you are considering whether to accept this gig, this job, this student, it helps to have that vision in place. You don't have to know the whole path, but if you can see that this opportunity feels like it moves toward your vision, it's a yes! If this other opportunity keeps you stuck where you are or working in a way you don't love, maybe it's a no or at least a take-this-with-your-eyes-open situation.

You don't have to see the whole path laid out in front of you. When your end goal is clear, and your first step is clear, that's all it takes to start.

THE LIVING VISION EXERCISE

Take some time to get comfortable. You'll need writing materials—a journal, a notepad, a pen. You'll need to be uninterrupted for 30 minutes or so. Turn off your notifications and put your phone in another room, so you can really find your way into your vision.

Take a few slow, deep breaths. Feel your feet on the floor, your body on the chair; feel your grounding on the earth. Pay attention to your breathing, to the miracle of your body doing what it is designed to do. Try to keep your focus on your breathing and in the present moment for a minute or so.

As you begin to feel relaxed, clear, and calm, imagine yourself a year, or three years, from now. Everything has been going so well for you. It's just the way you wanted it to be. Can you follow yourself in this vision through a normal day?

How do you wake up? Where are you in the world? Who is with you? How do you feel getting out of bed? What is your morning routine? When do you start to work? What kind of work are you doing? How do you feel doing it? Who are your colleagues? Who are your clients? How do you feel about them?

Take a look at your bank account in your vision. How much is in it, how does that feel to you? How hard are you working on this normal day? Are you constantly busy? Or is there downtime? What are you doing to take care of yourself? What are you doing for fun? What are you eating? Who is there with you?

Flesh this out in as much detail as you can. See the sights, smell the smells, hear the sounds. Let about half of it be completely believable and as much as half pure fantasy. It's OK if you don't see how you're going to get there yet. It's OK if you can't actually figure out how to make your bank account match the one in your vision, or how to make your schedule feel as luxurious. If you are living a perfectly normal day—six months, eighteen months, three years from now—and it feels exactly the way you'd like it to feel, what does that mean to you? Be specific and detailed.

This process will probably take 30 minutes or more, and it's time well spent. When you finish, you may have several pages of writing that describes the life and career you want to move toward, to manifest for yourself.

Because if you don't know where you're going, how will you know which route to take or when you've arrived?

REALITY CHECK

Next, let's look at your current life.

What are you doing right now that resonates with the vision you've just laid out? What are you doing already—*right now*—that you love to do and want more of? Is there a way to lean into that and do it more? What might that look like?

If that thing is teaching a certain kind of student, how could you attract more people like that? If it's performing in a certain way, how can you make more opportunities to do that? If it's your downtime activities—your weekend hikes or your quiet knitting nights—can you create more space to enjoy those? Could you monetize them by helping others to discover them? Is that a thing that might feel in alignment? It might not—but there's no harm in exploring an income stream outside music if you think you might enjoy it.

Now, let's look at the things you *dislike* in your current situation. Is it people? Is it your schedule? Is it email and busy work? Is it commuting? What things do you do every day that you hate doing, that don't feel enjoyable and easy and fun?

What could you do to minimize these in your life? Is there a way to outsource a task? Is there a way to use technology to make it easier? Is there something you could quit or could work toward replacing in your life?

I know how glib this sounds. Just get rid of the bad stuff; that's all you need to do. I know it's not always easy to make big changes happen. I know you still have to pay your rent. *I know.*

I also know that inertia is a powerful force. When you don't really pay attention or think about things, they don't change. Applying the power of your smart musician mind to a problem might actually solve it!

Here are some examples from my life:

- I hated agonizing over student schedules and trying to fit everyone in. Now I use an app called Calendly (there's a free version), and the participants in my groups can schedule their own private sessions within parameters I set.
- I was overwhelmed by my reed business and couldn't keep up with demand. So I hired a team of winders who process my cane and wind blanks for me. Every reed I sell is still hand-scraped by me, because that's the personal part, but I am happy to pay people to do the skilled but impersonal tasks of splitting, guillotining, pre-gouging, gouging, and winding.

- I love to write and to share my writing online. I hate to do hashtag research and find photos that match my text and format things differently for Instagram, Facebook, and my blog. I hired a virtual assistant to take care of the annoying parts of this process. Now I'm posting more often and more consistently, my work looks more professional, and I can see the benefits of that increased visibility in my business and in my engagement with my clients.
- I used to get to the end of my day feeling burned out, uncreative, and exhausted. I have reworked my schedule so I can take my mornings very slowly. I can run, practice, and write before I ever get onto calls with clients and students. I have limited the number of hours I spend teaching each day by moving toward group programs and constraining my teaching calendar.
- I used to accept orchestra jobs that looked great on paper—Yes! There was just enough time to get from place to place and show up for work!—with no attention to how energetically draining the repertoire or the commute would be. In our new post-pandemic times, I'm committed to being more mindful of how much and what kind of performing work I want to put on my calendar.

When you first create your Living Vision, it might seem impossibly distant. The gap between Current You and Dream You might feel insurmountable. This is normal.

So I invite you to take this second step and ask yourself: What could I do right now that would feel 5% *more* like the life I really want?

- I had a great feeling of spaciousness in my vision—big open rooms and minimal furnishings. In my actual life, I was sitting at a desk covered with clutter, with a music stand pulled in tightly on my right and an overflowing recycle bin behind me to my left. Twenty minutes of tidying made me feel more like the me I wanted to grow into.
- I had envisioned a close and warm family relationship, but looking around I found that everyone was on devices, ignoring each other. We implemented a regular afternoon tea break where we could check in with each other. It was so little, so easy to add, and so important!

If you look at your Vision and see clients that you love and look forward to working with, where are they in your current picture? Could you evolve your perception of your current students? (I sometimes get a lot from the exercise of putting myself in someone else's shoes and trying to see what they need, rather than what I want them to want.) Could you design an offer to draw more ideal people into your life? Could you let one terrible student go, with your blessings?

Fill your life with the things you want and reminders of the things you want, and look at concrete paths toward having those things. You don't need to see the whole path before you start. You don't need to snap your fingers and have the whole thing come true. It's a process of evolution, and you create the mutations that start that process!

Remember, you are already a musician. You know how to take a difficult thing and break it down into manageable tasks, how to make intuitive leaps and connections, and how to put in the work, bit by bit, until the problem is solved. What if you applied those skills, the ones you already have, to designing the career and the life you want?

I'm sure this has happened to you. In a lesson, or in the orchestra, you've had your teacher or conductor suggest something you hadn't considered. What if you played the line more like this? More like a light spring shower, more like a terrifying invasion, more like an echo? I'll bet you were effortlessly able to make that change; you have all the skills, you just hadn't thought of the idea.

That's the key here. Put in some energy now—*today*—toward having the idea, and you will know how to start moving toward it. It's not magic, it's you. *Start evolving.*

PRIVILEGE

"But Jennet," I can hear you crying. "I can't *afford* to make any changes now! I can't drop students; I can't turn down bad work. *Everything* is already so tight and so scarce that there's no room to breathe! It sounds easy for you but it isn't for me!"

I hear that.

Aside from my obvious privilege as a cis, white, straight-sized woman, I have the good fortune of being an excellent musician. I went to a top conservatory, and as much as I've been griping in this book about its lack of practical education, I can say that I was well-trained to play the oboe. The oboe itself has not been my obstacle.

More privilege: I had a pretty good scholarship so my loans were manageable and I paid them off quickly. I've been around a while now and am established enough in my portfolio career that I could afford to drop almost all of my teaching to make space to think and breathe. I am busy enough within my network of orchestra gigs that I can turn down the occasional un-fun job. I have my reed business and now my online programs to cushion most monetary blows;

even in lean months there is enough. I know this is not the case for everyone.

But I feel so passionately that it should be!

Artists and musicians should not be starving or struggling. You have so much talent, so much drive, so much potential. I promise that there is room out there for you to make your own vision a reality, and people who want what you can offer, if only you create it for them.

It's fair, though, and practical, to look at your own set of assets at this point. Where are you, *actually,* in the hierarchy of musicians or other artists in your area? There's a ranking by seniority in most freelance scenes, but also a ranking by ability and professionalism. Are there skills you don't have that you need? Is your personal demographic a limitation for you, in a way that it isn't for me? Limitations aren't stop signs; they are obstacles to notice and be aware of. You can do anything, but it doesn't hurt to acknowledge the real-world difficulties in play.

EVOLUTION, NOT REVOLUTION

Let's talk about how you might evolve.

What's your greatest limitation right now? Is it time, money, knowledge, or something else?

If it's knowledge or a skill that you lack, you can fix that! Who is teaching this? How could you find the information you need? How could you work around needing to learn? I don't know how to design a book, so I'm paying someone to create this one rather than spending my time learning software I'll only use once. But it's important to me to do my own bookkeeping and banking so I make the effort to understand those processes. It's worth taking a few minutes to analyze what you are missing and consider the benefits and costs of gaining that knowledge versus paying for someone else's help.

I love a really practical approach of listing out all of the things you do in a week. The tasks, the amount of time they occupy, the amount of return on investment, or ROI. (Your time and your excellent energy are always an investment). What is taking the most time? What costs you the most in terms of your energy? Where is your money coming from? If you need to reclaim some time, or earn more money, or free up your mental load to get better work done, what might you do?

Look for the low-hanging fruit. Chances are there is something in your calendar that is a net loss, something that takes more time and energy than it compensates you in return. Could you raise your rates or limit your time doing this thing? Could you just *stop* doing it?

Chances are that there is something that lights you up and energizes you. Can you monetize it, or raise your rates, or in some other way do more of it? On this purely practical level, can you see some things to tweak?

Everything isn't about money, right? Maybe you adore teaching a scholarship student who isn't paying you much, and you have some other students that suck the life out of you despite paying on time every week. You are allowed—encouraged!—to hold onto the things in your life that you love to do. But might there be a way to reshuffle some other streams? Look for a way to move toward a more relaxed, abundant, fulfilling life.

What if you designated one week per month as a studio week, and instead of giving lessons, you ran one or two group classes? You'd save hours of 1:1 teaching time, you'd give great content to your students, your income could stay the same or go up because of the increased value you are offering, and you'd reduce your 1:1 time with the students you don't love.

What if you restructured that teaching altogether, adding guest teacher slots and raising your rates? That way, you're supporting other teaching artists as well! What if you created an offering that brought new students in at a rate high enough to let a few old ones go?

Maybe you're doing a gig or a job you hate, earning some sort of hourly wage. What if you looked for a new job that you might actually love, even if it isn't musical?

Maybe your scarcity is around work time, because your kids are constantly home during this pandemic and you can't get away from them. Might there be a way to share these responsibilities? A childcare or home school pod, your spouse committing to some hours, you creating a "movie time" from 3 PM-5 PM where screens are fully allowed and you get to buckle down and work?

I know it feels overwhelming. There are so many steps involved in creating a new idea, starting a new business or side hustle, or even just making changes to what you have now.

Glance back at your Living Vision and spend a minute feeling the energy of the future that you dreamed of.

Now, spend a few minutes thinking about what your life might be like in a year if you don't take action. If you *don't* dig in and make some changes, what is that going to feel like? Is that what you want?

You get to choose.

FOCUS

It's important to focus.

It might appear that I am doing 16 things at a time all the time, and that impression would not be incorrect. Many aspects of my career, though, are running more or less on autopilot.

My reed business is busy, sometimes more so and sometimes less, but the processes and the workflow are well established. I'm not re-inventing the wheel, I'm just doing the work, and that work is slotted into my schedule in a way that works for me.

I am running two group programs simultaneously right now. Three, if you count Reed Club as a separate entity. But the energetic work of creating these programs, *designing* them, and launching and selling them has already happened.

Those processes were very energy intensive; they required all of my focus. But having run them before, I knew I could run them again. I love showing up to my classes and being able to just do what I do, as though I'm showing up to work and not as though I'm inventing something from scratch.

I send a weekly email, write a weekly blog post, and produce a weekly video. Here again, I have my workflow established, I know where these tasks fit in my week, and I have already worked through the start-up phases of these activities.

You might look at a well-established portfolio career and think you could never get so many interlocking pieces to interlock. You might think there's no way to build your career to such a successful place.

It's possible, but here's the key: build one thing at a time. Every day I get new ideas! New inspirations, things I *could* do for my groups or for other people or for myself. I think about group programs, about new offers, about new ways to help oboists and musicians. I think about new books I could write or new topics to explore.

But, and this is important, I do not chase every one of these ideas with reckless abandon. I know that staying on task and doing the job I told myself I was going to do this week is the only way to really get it done. I don't want to lose my new ideas, but I can't run around starting things every day and hope to actually support myself.

Starting things is *fun!* Finishing them, slogging through the *middle* of a project to the very end, can be hard and mostly ungratifying.

I have an *Idea Parking Lot.* This is a concept I heard of first from the fabulous Racheal Cook. My Idea Parking Lot is a Trello board, but it could exist in any app or in a notebook.

The important thing is that there's a set place to park your brilliant ideas where you know you can find them again. Not a bunch of random post-it notes, in other words, but a place you can come back to.

In my IPL, I flesh out a new idea as much as I can. Whatever brilliant thoughts I had about it while I was driving or running or listening to a podcast—I get them down. I think about whether this is a useful idea right now or not.

Generally, I let these ideas sit in the parking lot for a little while. Some of them get some real traction in my brain, so I return to them regularly and toss more details into them. And when I am ready to start something new, when I have a clear moment, or when I just can't ignore those great ideas anymore, I go back to my Idea Parking Lot and drive something off the lot.

The IPL is a great way to nurture my creativity, to explore both good and bad ideas, and a way to tuck them somewhere safe until I can really engage with them. Having ideas is not too hard for me, but the thought of losing one is terrifying. I want to capture them, and explore them when the hot flush of excitement has passed, and figure out what it would take to implement them, and make sure I can put in the energy to execute them successfully.

This is me speaking from my mid-40s, right? I have a lot going on—a family, a career, a house, a retirement account that is not really there yet. The discipline of trying to hold ideas instead of immediately acting on every one has been a long time in developing.

It's definitely true that in the past I've been guilty of starting something new *much too often* with no real strategic plan, and being limited in scope and execution because of that. I've been guilty of sitting on my bigger, scarier ideas until they sort of wisped away. So I want to encourage you to be thoughtful about this concept.

You can't do everything at once. It's important to give your ideas a real shot at success by allowing yourself the space to dig into them and get them off the ground. And it's also important to try them! Too much action leads to thrashing around, but too much thought and preparation can lead to not starting.

I want to invite courage here: courage to start a new project even if it feels messy and uncertain; courage to commit to the thing you are starting and give it a real chance. Where is that line for you?

WHO IS YOUR TEAM?

I have one final thought for this chapter: Who do you need on your side to help you along the way?

I have a mastermind group of four other amazing women. We meet each week to support each other and help with challenges that come up in our businesses. Our fields are different, but our struggles are relatable, and it's great to have a team to bounce ideas off.

I have a mastermind partner, another woman working a music-based business. We have a similar audience, but we engage with them differently, we're not in competition with each other, and we meet every other week to discuss what is coming up for us and to set goals and report on them.

I have a business coach. I'm in a group coaching program with a ton of fantastic, high-level musicians who are all working to pivot their careers in similar ways to me. We meet on weekly calls and have a group to bounce ideas around in.

I have a CPA who understands the financial ins and outs of my business and takes my calls when I have questions.

I have a husband who supports the business I am running and the creative work I am trying to do. He's a wonderful, engaged parent and has done far more than half of the hands-on childrearing in this family.

I have a group of amazing, creative artist friends in a variety of disciplines. We meet once a week to talk about our creative lives.

It's really important to surround yourself with people who support your ambitions and who have some ambitions of their own. Remember those crabs in the pot? Lots and lots of musicians still live in the mindset of scarcity, the idea that creating work outside of traditional pathways is selling out, the sense that marketing and hustle are vulgar. If these are the kinds of people you spend most of your time with, it can be really difficult and frightening to move forward.

Who is on your team? What do you need that you don't have? Do you need a peer group? A mentor? A coach? A cheering squad? Identifying the lack is always the right first step toward filling it!

READY TO GO?

I hope that at this point you have some clarity around what you want and who you need, and a few potential action steps planned.

Now that you have your Vision, your Reality, the first steps of your Evolution, and your Team identified, you're ready to go, right? Ready to build an empire? I hope so!

But many people get stuck right at this point, and a huge trigger for musicians is visibility. Let's look at that next.

12

Visibility

I went to an audition shortly before the COVID lockdowns started. I didn't even want the job. There's some part of me that isn't fully done taking auditions—that still sort of wants to make a big change of some sort, that maybe secretly still believes that this time the gatekeepers will let me through—so I sent in my resume in a moment of weakness.

Sitting in the group warm-up room with all of the shockingly young people who were competing against me, I knew it had been a mistake to come. One of those baby oboists looked at me hard, and said, "Oh, I know you! Aren't you the one who makes all those reed videos?"

Now, I love to be recognized, but I noticed that she did not immediately say, "I love your videos! They've helped me so much!" or anything else like that.

So in my head, I made it mean that she was judging me for making educational videos instead of winning auditions, instead of being a real performer, instead of following the narrow path to success that we have been led to believe is the only one.

Isn't this ridiculous?

Between my audition nerves and my discomfort at being seemingly older than the other people in the room, I let myself feel disempowered as an artist and mentally trashed all of my life's successes. This one girl—who was probably feeling some audition nerves, too, who was probably not at her social best, either—derailed my whole day, and I'm still thinking about this interaction over a year later.

Visibility is a life's work.

We get slowly comfortable with one level of it, and then flinch at the next level, over and over and over. But we don't become musicians so that we can shrink into the background! Whether your overall goal is to have a performing career, a thriving teaching studio, or to compose works that get played, your authority and talent have to be seen or no one will ever know to hire you.

Being visible—being known and noticed—in your field is such an important aspect of building a career. It's nice when that publicity comes from outside, when someone else brags about you first, but sitting back and waiting for the world to recognize your brilliance all on its own is probably a recipe for disappointment. You have to help them to find you.

This, by the way, is called marketing. There are dozens of books, videos, and online courses designed to help you get better at it. It is an essential skill. For me, though, it was impossible to think like a marketer before I got over my fear of visibility. I couldn't put myself in someone else's shoes when I was too busy quaking in my own. The first step toward becoming an expert marketer of yourself, your product, and your performances is to dare to be seen at all. That's the focus of this chapter.

WHY IS VISIBILITY SO SCARY?

As a musician, especially a classical musician, you've been trained your whole life to be perfect. Mistakes are unacceptable. The pinnacle of success is when you get your rendition of a piece as close as possible to the CD, which is, of course, perfect. There's only a little bit of margin for interpretive choice—everything else seems to be objectively right or wrong. It can be stifling to feel that this is the standard you have to reach, and that everyone is judging you.

Additionally, we've been trained to not make enemies. We know that the classical music world is small, and that we have to be well-liked to work. In an orchestra, we're trained to be extra polite to the patrons and the donors, to keep our conversational topics neutral, to never say anything negative about our colleagues or to mention that Republicans are a bunch of hypocritical monsters. We are taught not to offend. Because if we offend anyone, we might lose work. We might be fired. The money might go away from the orchestra.

The message we internalize from all of this is that it is dangerous to be seen.

So musicians—traditionally—go to work and do their job, but they hesitate to put themselves out there. To share their playing in more visible ways is frightening. Someone might see them being imperfect! Musicians tend to keep their opinions very neutral in public. Can't alarm the donors! And musicians tend not to admit to each other that they have ideas, ambitions, or creativity beyond the job at hand, lest other musicians see them as less serious.

I hate this.

I hate these attitudes, which I also have internalized. I hate thinking that it's not appropriate to be fully myself, to state my opinions, and to be visible as a musician, as a creative person, as a human. And I don't believe that this fear around visibility is serving us, as artists, any more in this day and age.

WHY IS VISIBILITY SO IMPORTANT?

We've been taught to play our instruments onstage and to not worry our pretty little heads about the business side of the orchestra business. But what happens when you want to create a program for yourself?

I've given far too many recitals and chamber music concerts to empty halls. Understanding how to reach out to the people in your community and how to interest them in your artistry is a key ingredient that was not covered in my conservatory education.

What is it about your program, about your colleagues, about you that is going to get people out of their houses to hear live music? It's almost certainly not a dry listing of the pieces and composers you've programmed; it's a conversation about *why* these pieces, *why* this event, *why* they should care.

When I advertise what I'm doing, I put myself in the shoes of my audience and think about what would interest them. It's not how hard I've worked in my practice room, or how Beethoven went deaf—it's the story behind the music, it's the emotional impact they might get from hearing it, it's how this work is relevant to our own time.

This goes for your orchestra concerts as well. You know all that messaging about how classical music is dying? What if you were an ambassador for your orchestra? What if people could see you, out in the world, a living, breathing person who has committed your life to this "dying" art?

Again, we've been trained to stay in our lane, show up for our rehearsals and concerts, and shut up about it. I've seen plenty of musicians gripe about seeing the hall half empty for a concert—and lay all of the blame squarely on Management.

After all, the music director is supposed to program compelling concerts that attract traditional donors who want traditional repertoire and bring in newer, younger audiences with newer, hipper music. The marketing department is supposed to be putting this material in front of potential concert-goers in a compelling way, so that the public clamors to attend. The patron services department is supposed to be delighting them when they do come, and the development department solicits them for donations afterward to keep the whole thing afloat.

And sure, those are all jobs that people are doing. But in another, more urgent, sense it is *everyone's* job to make a concert an exciting experience. We need to be telling our friends and neighbors about the performances we give. We need to be raving about them on social media. We need to be a part of the solution. When we show up on stage, we give a great performance. And when we see patrons leaving the hall, we need to be engaging with them there as well!

If you want to have a career that you love—if you want to attract clients who really resonate with your message, if you want to lean into your own creativity and monetize it—you need to be noticed. The Internet has changed the world, and now there are no gatekeepers to keep you from being visible! The job now is to cut through the clutter to be seen.

If everyone is able to share themselves online, what brings people to you? It's almost certainly not your skill at threading the needle and being inoffensive to everyone. It's not how perfectly you can disappear into the texture of a viola section. It's how compelling your message is and how you can make it stand out online.

No one wants to come to just any violinist for lessons, they want to come to *the* violinist, the one they have gotten to know. No one books a solo performer just because she can play all the notes correctly. It's because she has something to say with her music and with her marketing and with her voice.

Don't be beige. Dare to show up in full color. It's more interesting for your audience, and it's more fun for you, too!

WHAT IF THEY DON'T LOVE YOU?

Here's the downside of being visible, of course. Sometimes when people see you, they won't like what they see. You might get comments, reactions, responses that are unwelcome. Things that trigger you. Things that upset you and make you want to hide. Sometimes you'll get haters.

It doesn't even take a hater. Remember how twigged I got at that audition just because a person who recognized me didn't rave about me?

I know people whose fear of the haters, or even of well-intentioned comments from colleagues and fans, is so intense that they won't start. I know people who won't even post on social media lest they be seen, who might share an inoffensive quote over an image, but wouldn't dream of sharing actual words from their own heads. I know people who put their playing on YouTube but only on private settings, to keep for themselves or to share with a tightly curated circle of safe supporters.

A coach (it was Tracy, and you can read more about her after this chapter), once helped me get past some of this fear by asking, "*Who, specifically, do you think is going to judge you?*"

When I thought this through, I imagined three or four people who might be negative about my choices. And then I thought further and realized that none of these people mattered! They weren't doing what I was doing. They weren't even people who might imminently hire me! They were just judgy colleagues who weren't striving to put their opinions and their work out into the world. And who didn't, in fact, say anything about my online presence.

If you, too, are getting stuck trying to start, could you ask yourself who the voices in your head represent? Are they people you actually need to listen to? Do their points have any validity? What could you say to them in response?

Could you notice your own reaction to other people you've seen trying things? When you see someone announce a new business, or advertise a performance, or brag about their students, do you grin nastily to yourself and decide that their ambition is invalid? I bet you don't. If you're like me, it's thrilling to see people using their talents and breaking new ground. Don't you think people will be happy for you, too?

When you do share something, and when you do receive feedback, what do you need to do with it? Every response you get, positive or negative, tells you something. Should you change your direction, your musical interpretations, your choices based on what other people think?

Any response you get to your work tells you how it is landing. The people who love it will tell you so. The people who dislike it will, too, and then you get to decide: Is this someone I need to listen to? Is this someone who knows about the field I'm in, about the work I'm doing? Is this someone who would be a customer, if only I had done a better job of reaching them? Or is this someone I'd never work with anyway, someone who doesn't want what I do? Is this someone whose opinion of my work matters, or is my work just not for that person?

If anyone tried to sell me a foolproof method of, say, throwing a football in a perfect spiral, I would not pay for that. I don't care about the ball, I don't want to throw a spiral. That's not for me. They might be the best football-throwing-teacher on the entire Internet, and I can respect that, but it's not for me. Similarly, you may encounter people who are not your ideal audience. It's not for them. You don't have to worry about them.

HOW DO YOU START?

It's crucially important to find your audience, to find your people. And the way to start is to start.

What is your platform? Is it social media, like Facebook, Instagram, LinkedIn? Is it videos or a vlog on YouTube? Is it long form writing, like Medium? Do you have an email list? (You should definitely have an email list.)

Try stating a belief on your chosen platform. Try stating an unpopular opinion, and explaining why you hold it. Try inviting people to engage with you around your area of interest. Put something out that matters, and invite responses. When you get them, engage with them. And then tomorrow? Do it again.

It's worth being brave. It's worth being consistent. Because your voice matters.

SHARE THE MESSY MIDDLE

Here's what the kids are doing over on Instagram. They are making "practice accounts" and sharing their work in progress. They are sharing snippets of pieces, little technical etudes, minute-long snatches of what is happening. They are sharing the messy middle.

I adore this.

The first magic in this is that the process of recording yourself—listening to what you're doing, making judgments for yourself about what is good enough to share, trying again to make the snippet represent where you are in the journey—this process is making you better.

The second magic is that seeing your brave journey makes other people feel braver. And more people sharing makes a community. There are so many musicians on Instagram putting up bits of music—tiny performances created in their bedrooms and offices. And they see each other and hear each other.

How many live performances can you go to? Even before the pandemic there probably weren't more than a few programs available in a given week in your town or city. On Instagram, you can hear players every day.

The third magic is that within this community it feels safe to be vulnerable. Every person I have seen says, at some point in the journey, "This isn't as good as I want it to be, but it's the best I have today." This includes real professionals holding major orchestral chairs, and it includes middle schoolers.

Everyone works through these feelings of frustration and disappointment. When you listen, sometimes you can't even tell what they're talking about—the playing sounds beautiful. Or in the case of the 14-year-olds, it at least sounds representative. The tiny flaws you hear in your own playing are real, and they are worth working on, but in many cases they don't distract from the work you are trying to share.

The final magic is that this community is *kind*. Sometimes there's feedback, if the person asked for it—but I have never once seen a nasty, trolling response of any sort on one of these practice posts. The humanity of the person sharing their work is honored.

I struggle with social media sometimes, too: how much to post, how to be visible, what to keep back, what to give generously, and what to save for paying clients. But I love and admire the community of Instagram Practice Accounts.

Go and look at #oboepractice. Or #100daysofpractice. Or get creative with your hashtag search, because the kids sure are. What if you put some playing out there yourself? What would it feel like to just share something, even imperfectly?

TALL POPPY SYNDROME

I first heard of Tall Poppy Syndrome on a podcast. It's not something I grew up knowing about, but I recognized it right away. In some cultures, it's expected that you will keep yourself small and not outshine the people around you. The Tall Poppy is the one that gets cut down. It's dangerous to stand out, dangerous to be noticed.

I would suggest that classical music is such a culture. There are superstars, sure, but the rest of us are supposed to stay small: section players shouldn't stick out, second flutists should be seen and not heard.

But what if that's not enough for you?

The idea that someone else might see you being ambitious, might see you being creative, might see you dreaming is frightening. But will anything bad actually happen?

I believe there is room for more than one artist in a niche. I believe that you have it in you to be a tall, beautiful poppy, and that when more of us decide to flourish and grow, it's better for everyone. The more the general public sees musicians and creative artists thriving in the world, making comfortable incomes, being fulfilled and happy, the more artists (and patrons of the arts) will join us!

If Thoreau's statement is true, that "the mass of men lead lives of quiet desperation," I'd suggest that allowing more people access to creativity, passion, and agency in their lives is a way to reduce that desperation.

Let us *see* you!

SPOTLIGHT ON A CAREER

TRACY FRIEDLANDER

Tracy Friedlander is a business coach helping artists and creatives turn their passion and expertise into a 6-figure methodology. She is the host of the podcast *Crushing Classical.*

TRACY, HOW WOULD YOU DESCRIBE YOUR CURRENT WORK?

I am a coach who helps musicians, artists, and creatives discover how they can turn their unique expertise in their passion into a full-time income.

HOW DID YOU START DOING WHAT YOU DO?

I began my career in the traditional sense, with my eyes set on winning a job in an orchestra. I was on the audition path throughout my 20s and early 30s, all the while building a busy freelance career. In 2016, I hit a wall, realizing that while I had created a performing career, I wanted more.

I set off to find out what that meant—and began by starting a podcast called *Crushing Classical,* interviewing musicians who have created unique careers outside the traditional path.

Over the next few years, I learned as much as I could

about building an online business, and in 2019, I started helping musicians with their businesses online.

As all careers should, my business evolved as I worked with people and realized my favorite problems to solve. The more people I worked with, the more I realized my favorite people were the ones who had big ideas about what was possible in their careers. People who were willing to stand up and share their expertise with their own unique twist based on their personal experience and point of view.

There's power—and real money—in discovering how you can share your expertise, turn it into a business, and create your own creative economy.

WHAT DO YOU LOVE ABOUT YOUR WORK?

I love helping creatives realize that they have a depth of knowledge from their own curiosity, education, and experience that can actually turn into significant income—especially income that doesn't have a limit and is not tied to trading hours for dollars.

This is a foreign concept to most creatives, and when they discover how they can do it, it not only blows their mind, they gain a newfound confidence and excitement about what they do. That is definitely my favorite part!

WHAT IS THE MOST CHALLENGING ASPECT OF IT FOR YOU?

I have to pick one?

Business is super challenging. All the time I am faced with doing things that make me uncomfortable. But I know that in order to grow as a business owner (I mean, human!) I have to do things that take me outside my comfort zone.

I seek out these opportunities because comfort is definitely the path to career stagnation. But if I had to pick just one thing, it's that usually I want things to go faster. Having patience is my most challenging thing. Slow and steady wins the race, as they say.

WHAT BARRIERS DID YOU HAVE TO OVERCOME TO GET TO WHERE YOU ARE?

I'll be totally honest: the biggest barrier I had when I first started was what people thought of me. Would they think I was a "real" musician anymore if I was a business owner? Would people know what I do? Would they get it? Would I still feel like a "real" musician?

All of these things were related to my attachment to an identity I thought I wanted—and that I thought defined me. I finally got over that in a huge way. What I discovered is this: no label defines you, and an identity that you think defines you can hold you back.

This can keep you from saying or doing the things you know need to be said or done to make changes in your own life, career, or industry. I have seen too many people afraid of what other people think about them to the point where they become incredibly disempowered.

WHAT ADVICE WOULD YOU GIVE TO SOMEONE WHO WANTED TO HAVE A CAREER LIKE YOURS?

Do your research, get support from someone who can guide you in the right direction and help you with a strategy. Trying to do everything yourself causes things to take far longer than they need to take.

And start immediately! You know what they say: "The best time to plant a tree is 20 years ago; the second best time to plant one is today!"

IS THERE ANYTHING YOU WOULD LIKE TO ADD?

As musicians, we are trained that the only path to a career is getting a job, either in an orchestra or in an educational institution. This is so limiting.

Waiting to be chosen is no way to live. If you decide not to wait, a world opens up for you. Then, if you go for an opportunity in which you need to be chosen by others (a committee, for example), you're no longer attached to the idea that, "This needs to work and they have to pick me".

You can be unattached to the outcome and you can be not desperate. There's nothing more disempowering than having all of your eggs in one basket.

What I want for all musicians is that they can see that they have a whole world of options. It's just that outside of the main two options I listed above in the traditional path, the other options need to be created by you. That's the hard part. But it's so worth it!

13

You Get to Choose

Is your goal, ultimately, to make all of the money you will ever need and then retire and glide effortlessly into your life of leisure? To reset your life to the most perfect version of itself, after which you can rest and just let it run?

I can't speak for you, but that's not *my* goal.

For me the goal is always *flow*. I'm addicted to this state in which I'm working at something just a little bit difficult. I love losing myself in a piece of creative writing, in a bit of technical practicing. I love to be in *flow* in performance. I love to have or to facilitate an *Aha!* moment while I'm teaching.

All of my career choices so far have been made in pursuit of *flow*, and my favorite times are when I am there. I don't know that sitting back and watching my Roth IRA increase in value is going to take me into that flow state. In fact, I am quite sure that it is not.

I imagine that I will continue to create new offers, new ideas, new programs, new performances, and new writings forever. The dream life in my Living Vision is not based in Indiana, but it's also not based in some sort of Eden where I no longer have to work. It's just that I'll be working with ever greater, more interesting, more challenging clients! I'll be crafting more interesting and challenging performances! Right now I'm trying to build a business foundation that keeps the money flowing so I can keep challenging myself more and more interestingly.

Obviously, though, my dream isn't your dream. What is it that *you* want to be doing? Is a *flow* state what you want? What creates that for you?

What would your ideal amount of work be in your imagined future? How would you balance playing, teaching, creating, leisure, family life—and anything else that needs to be in balance for your life to light you up? What is your optimal level of challenge? What do you want to be creating and how all-encompassing do you want it to be?

BALANCE

Balance is important, and not talked about enough in our field, and also impossible to actually achieve. Let's talk about this for a second.

In everyone's life there is a conversation to be had about work-life balance. All the business and self-help books talk about ways to make sure you are present to your family and friends in addition to your career. And that's important, but in some ways musician-entrepreneurs have even more masters to serve.

Family and work, sure. By work, I mean the day-to-day version of showing up to rehearse, to teach, to do your day job. But in addition to these, musicians contend with their artistic and creative practices on their own. Musician-entrepreneurs also need to be involved with the creativity of building out their new income streams.

We need to feel that we are involved with our artistry. Even if we are already amazing—plenty good enough to keep showing up for rehearsals and concerts, and without aspirations beyond that—it's a given that we need to continue to engage with our craft just to maintain that appropriate level.

Reed players still need to spend time making and adjusting their reeds, and everyone needs to stay in touch with their instrumental fundamentals. If you are at an earlier stage in your career, and on the audition circuit or building your solo visibility, you are constantly focused on your repertoire, your playing, and your skills.

For years, before my daughter was born, my playing was really my only focus. The things I added to the mix, like my reed business and teaching, took a clear backseat to the work of developing myself into the best musician I could be. This single-minded focus is normal for musicians. It's what makes us such superheroes. But it can also be what keeps us trapped, tunnel-visioning along the narrow path our younger selves envisioned toward success. I wish I had been better able to zoom out and see the bigger picture earlier on. I could have moved much more quickly toward the joy of my current life.

But there is no shame in being who we are, where we are.

CYCLES

There may not ever be such a thing as perfect balance. Things come up, projects might force you to put the rest of your life on a back burner for a while. But no one is better suited to manage all of this than you, a musician. You know how to take a project that feels insurmountable and break it down into manageable steps. You know how to zoom in and out, looking at the big picture and the tiny details that go into it. You know that there are a variety of approaches to learning things: sometimes you listen, sometimes you run through just to assess where you are, sometimes you go right into the technical work, sometimes you leave the specific project alone and just practice fundamentals or do some research to change your approach.

Musicians are trained to be project-based: each orchestra concert is its own project, every school semester is a project, every recital or recording project is a project. We are accustomed to the cycle of starting something new, working through the middle, and culminating in a performance, whether that cycle stretches over three days or six months.

We are used to the fact that every day doesn't look the same, because every day holds a different aspect of the project. Some days are more work than others, depending on where they fall in the cycle of a project and how many projects are going simultaneously.

Sometimes you just have to warm up and get to an easy pops concert. Sometimes you need to do a full recital run-through, and also pick up your programs from the printer, and also schedule a piano tuning, and also have a rehearsal for someone else's thing, and teach three lessons.

Instead of thinking about work-life balance, I like to think in terms of cycles.

I have a daily energy cycle, my circadian rhythm. I know that I am freshest and most creative in the morning, so I generally don't schedule clients or classes during that time. Rather, I keep it open to write and to practice. I try to start the day with exercise to further energize this creative time.

After lunch, my energy shifts. I like to react rather than creating, so I do most of my best teaching and coaching during this period. I try to take some time in the late afternoon to rest, to meditate, to have a treat. By evening, my energy is waning so I make reeds and watch Internet television if I'm not at a rehearsal or a concert.

I have a monthly cycle, my infradian rhythm. I know that there are weeks when I will have less energy and weeks when the ideas are exploding out of me and I feel like a superhero. I'm not especially good at predicting these, especially now in midlife, but I'm getting better at accepting them and harnessing them for what they can offer me.

Every project has its own cycle, and the more I can predict what those look like and when the intensity will peak, the better I can plan around them.

As a freelance musician and creator, balance doesn't always happen on a daily basis. Any day might be too busy, too unbalanced in one direction or another. I've mentioned before my tendency to put concerts on my calendar that technically fit, with no attention to how hard they are going to *feel* in the moment.

I try to look at my balance in terms of a week view, or even a month view. If Mondays are a disaster because of students, maybe Wednesdays could be light and focused on content creation. If this week is crazy because it's a big orchestra concert and also the week before juries (so your students are insane), maybe next week is for taking naps and peacefully practicing fundamentals.

But you get to choose.

The more income streams you have in your portfolio career, the more stability you have within your network of career options, the more you can choose what you want your life to look like and the more you can opt to keep your days, weeks, and months balanced. What does it look like for you, ideally? You get to choose.

THRIVE LIST

I have to pay attention to my body and my mind. I know what I need to thrive because I've created a Thrive List.

When I start to feel overwhelmed, when I start to snap unreasonably at my family, I know to check back and notice what's missing. My Thrive List is simple.

In no particular order it is:

- Sleep
- Exercise
- Practice
- Write
- Solitude
- Food

When I start to fall apart emotionally or physically, I go back to my list and prioritize what is lacking.

What's on *your* Thrive List?

THE HAPPIEST MUSICIAN

To keep the big picture in mind, look back at your Living Vision every now and then. No need to check in weekly, nothing evolves quite that fast, but maybe every quarter or twice a year.

Is any of it coming true? Are you beginning to feel an evolution toward the feelings it evokes? Is there anything in there that you can now see how to bring into your life? Perhaps when you first wrote it you tackled a bit of the low-hanging fruit. Perhaps some other elements have now begun to hang low.

I'd encourage you to fully rewrite that vision once a year. Because as you do things, as you feel what they are like, your vision will evolve. You may begin to want something different. The point of that Living Vision document is definitely not to lock you into what last year's version of You decided was a life goal. The vision is Living, which means it can change. At any time, you can sink into your breathing and dream your life anew. And you can begin to evolve toward that new dream.

You do not have to wait for a big orchestra to choose you, you do not have to wait for the phone to ring. The age of gatekeepers is over. You are allowed to have agency in your musical, artistic, creative, and financial path!

I think the key to being The Happiest Musician is to get as clear as possible about what you want your life to be like. Brainstorm ways to bring elements of that life to you right now, and take manageable, enjoyable action steps toward the full picture. It is amazing what you can do with the education, hard and soft skills, and work ethic you already have. You can create a life that is creatively, financially, and personally satisfying, and I want that for you.

The more musicians, artists, and creative people are able to *rise,* the more possibility exists for us all. The more our society can view the arts as real work, can see artists as successful people, can see working musicians flourish, the easier it will be for the next generation to move into a world of opportunity and ease.

This is my message: Be willing to take some agency in your career and your life, and you, too, can be The Happiest Musician!

Epilogue

If I might go "meta" for a moment, I'd love to point out that I am living my message in real time right now.

You've just finished reading the newest facet of my own portfolio career. I've been blogging for a long time, but I have never been an "author" before. This is a new role I've created for myself, just in the past year.

I'm writing this epilogue in September of 2021. When I look back at my year-end journaling from 2020, I see no mention of this book. It came to me as an idea in January. I wrote the first draft in February. And I've been working ever since to make it a reality.

Like all creative enterprises, it has two aspects: *doing* it and *thinking* about it.

Writing the book was an enjoyable creative challenge. I put all of the words down, then looked at them all again and changed the order, structured and restructured the book, had some people read it and give me feedback, and then I worked again to improve it.

During the process, I got a lot of clarity around what I was really trying to share. It's amazing how writing words on a page, in black and white, forces you to get concrete and clear on your own concepts.

I started with a basic outline and a vague idea. During my writing process, with the help of my readers and editors and friends, I *evolved* my book into one that I hope has value for you!

I created a structure for my writing. Well, I found a *community* and a *structure* that helped me, and I wrote every day with a group of people who kept me accountable. Turns out, if you show up every day for an hour, the work gets done!

I also got *help.* So many generous people have read for me, edited for me, and talked me through the self-publishing and launch process. (Read the acknowledgments in my "Thanks" section below to learn about the people who helped me most.)

As scary as it was to think of myself as writing a book, I *started.* And then I just kept going. Once I was in motion, it was easier to keep working than not to.

But stepping into the role of Author—and into a voice of authority on the concepts addressed here—was a different challenge.

I worked through different versions of Imposter Syndrome around this. Why should anyone listen to me? Who do I think I am to talk about Classical Music in this way? I'm not even famous!

Then, as I got a little further along: What will people *think* of me when I publish this? What if they don't like it? Why *should* they like it, anyway?

Now that I'm close to publishing it, the voices in my head are louder than ever. Who is going to pay attention to this self-published piece of drivel? No one should!

Do those voices sound familiar? These are the voices that want you to keep playing small, the voices that want you to stick to the plan, stay in your lane, and keep working patiently and quietly until someday you get noticed and acknowledged.

I hear these same voices every time I create something new. I hear them, I fear them, and then I move on past them. This is the life I have; this is my portfolio career. New things are scary, *and* change is good. I see myself helping people. This book, and my career coaching practice, represent my next path to doing so.

If anything you have read here is inspiring or helpful, or supports you in building the project, the career, or the life you want, *that* is what I want for you. I want you to bring your magic to the world. I want you to *thrive!*

Thanks

It felt so easy to write the first draft of this book. It poured out of me. There were things I needed to say and they came right onto the page. I figured I would have it published in three or four weeks.

But turning a burst of inspiration into an actual book that *means* something is much harder, and this was a journey I had never walked before. It has taken an entire village of readers, editors, commenters, helpers, coaches, and cheerleaders to bring it to this place. I am warmed by the generosity of the world.

I have to thank Joseph Sowa and Alexandra Gardner for not laughing in my face when they read the very earliest drafts. I have to thank Gala Aranaga for her phenomenal help and time and enthusiasm and support as we began to turn it a little more into a book. I need to thank my mid-project beta readers, Lillian Reed and Carl Colvin. Steve Peha, who carried me across the finish line and designed the beautiful cover and interior. All of the members of Akimbo's Writing in Community Workshop and the souls who showed up every weekday morning to write together and to keep *me* on track.

My coach, Jennifer Rosenfeld, for the original spark, for her belief in me, and for her calm presence as I worked through my terror of this project. The warm support of Susan Blackwell at exactly the right moment in my process. Danny Ziemann, for talking to me for hours about publishing and production. These people—my friends and my mentors—have been encouraging, helpful, and have offered their expertise and time so generously. I needed every bit of that generosity.

Thank you to my contributors—phenomenal musicians and entrepreneurs in their own right—Sean McNeely, Renée-Paule Gauthier, Jessica Wilkins, Amanda McIntosh, Tracy Friedlander, Shawna Lake, Rob Knopper. Thank you to the amazing Elizabeth Rowe for her beautiful work at the front of the book.

And thank you to *you* for reading. I love the oboe, but it takes an audience to turn practicing into performance. I loved writing this book, but without a reader it's just an academic exercise, something I did in my office rather than something that was real. This book is for you, and I so appreciate you being here to receive it. Thank you.